Microsoft Excel 2003
Interactive Trainin

GW01191891

Summary of Contents

i

www.tsinteractive.com

ISBN-10: 1905707339
ISBN-13: 9781905707331

Printed in England
First Printing: June 2007

Published by C.B.Learning under the imprint of TS Interactive

C.B.Learning
205 Formans Road
Sparkhill
Birmingham B11 3AX
www.tsinteractive.com
enquiries@tsinteractive.com

Interactive Training: The CD-ROM

Excel 2003 Interactive Training Pack is a comprehensive package to help you learn Excel 2003. The CD-ROM expands on everything you see in the book, delivered in an engaging, interactive manner that stimulates learning.

▷ Insert the CD-ROM

If you need any help during installation, please refer to the "Troubleshooting the CD-ROM" section on page 173.

You will be welcomed by your instructor for the course, Ryan Doolittle. You hear Ryan explaining various concepts and providing demonstrations throughout the course.

The instructor is fully certified and has vast relevant experience in the subject

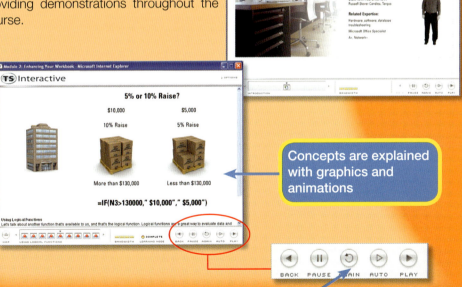

Concepts are explained with graphics and animations

Simple controls allow you to repeat lessons to make sure you fully understand them, or skip parts you are already comfortable with

Demonstrations and Hands-on Labs

▷ **Demonstrations guide you through each part of the course.**

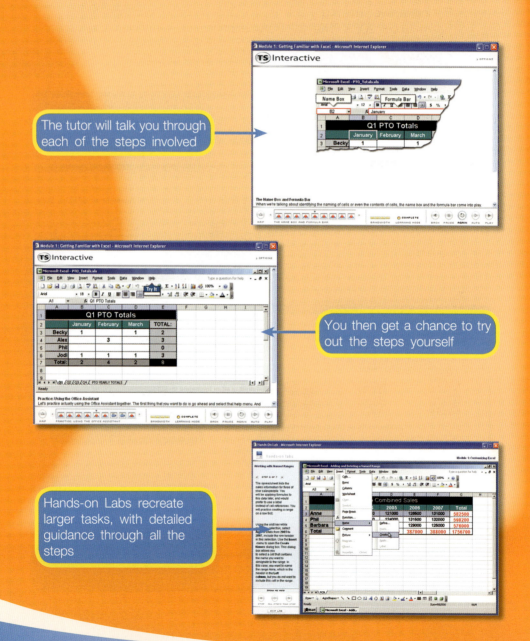

The tutor will talk you through each of the steps involved

You then get a chance to try out the steps yourself

Hands-on Labs recreate larger tasks, with detailed guidance through all the steps

Progress Tracker

▷ **Progress is recorded on the opening screen.**

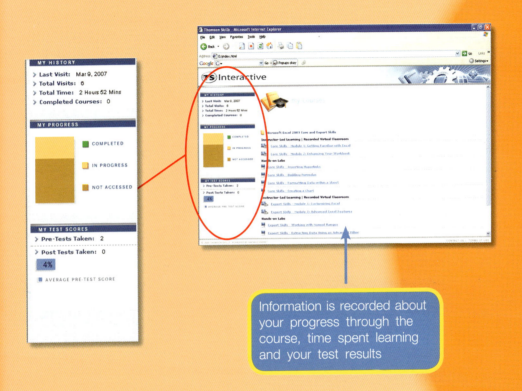

Information is recorded about your progress through the course, time spent learning and your test results

Navigation

▷ **Navigation round the course is simple and intuitive.**

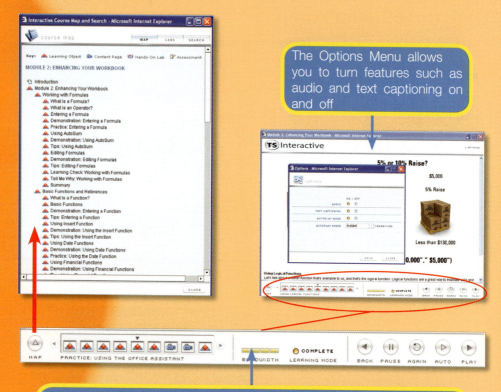

The Options Menu allows you to turn features such as audio and text captioning on and off

The Navigation Bar at the base of each screen during the course provides access to a map and easy navigation to all areas of the module

Assessment

▷ At the start of the course you take a "Pre-test". This will assess your knowledge and identify the areas of the course you need to study.

At the end of the test choose between "Complete" or "Personal" to determine whether the whole course is displayed, or simply the areas where further study is needed

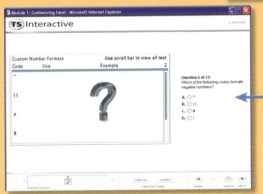

Questions typically follow a multiple choice format

Following completion of the test, all answers are fully explained

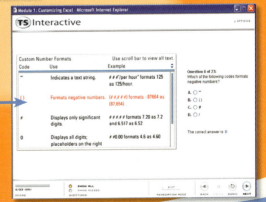

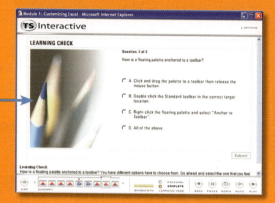

Periodic "Learning Checks" help gauge progress

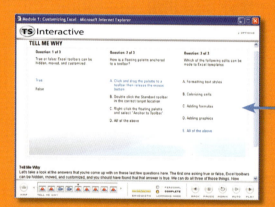

Immediately after each "Learning Check" is a section "Tell Me Why". The instructor talks in detail through the answers to highlight the key points

The end of module assessment points out areas where more study is required

Contents

Module 2: Enhancing the Workbook — 49

Microsoft Excel 2003 Expert Skills

Module 4: Advanced Excel Features 137

Microsoft Excel 2003 Basic Skills

Module 1: Getting Familiar with Excel

This module provides an introduction to the many exciting, timesaving features of Excel, an overview of the Excel application window, and the skills necessary to create a powerful workbook.

Objectives

Upon completing this module, you will be able to:

- ✔ Identify toolbar shortcuts and menu commands
- ✔ Navigate the Excel application window
- ✔ Open and create workbooks
- ✔ Enter and format text
- ✔ Insert, delete, and copy cells, rows, columns, and worksheets
- ✔ Freeze and unfreeze rows and columns
- ✔ Hide and unhide rows and columns
- ✔ Merge cells
- ✔ Define styles
- ✔ Use the AutoFill option

Outline

The module contains these lessons:

- Basic Features
- Opening and Creating a Workbook
- Entering and Formatting Text
- Managing Cells, Rows, Columns, and Worksheets

Basic Features

In this lesson, you will learn to identify the various parts of the Excel screen.

Objectives

Upon completing this lesson, you will be able to:

- ✔ Identify the options available on the Menu bar
- ✔ Identify various toolbars and their functions
- ✔ Identify rows, columns, and cells
- ✔ Navigate the Excel application window
- ✔ Use the Office Assistant

Title and Menu Bars

Microsoft Excel provides you with a variety of ways to complete functions. Before you create your first worksheet, you should be familiar with the Title and Menu bars.

Title Bar

The Title bar contains the title of the worksheet on which you are working. The Title bar is helpful when you are working with several different worksheets and it is necessary to differentiate between them.

The second important section of the Title bar contains the Control menu. The Control menu, located in the far-left corner of the Title bar, is activated only when it is clicked. Click this section of the Title bar to display sizing options, such as minimise and maximise, as well as the option to close the worksheet.

The far-right corner of the Title bar provides the same features as the Control menu, but in a more easily accessible format. You can close, minimise, or maximise the window using the three buttons shown in this corner.

Menu Bar

The Menu bar is located directly below the Title bar. From left to right, the Menu bar options are:

File Menu - From the File menu, you can complete basic operations, such as creating, opening, saving, and printing a workbook.

Edit Menu - The Edit menu contains a portion of the workbook-proofing tools. From this menu, you can undo mistakes, move and copy worksheets, find instances of words in the worksheet, and perform many other tasks.

View Menu - The View menu allows you to change the way you view an Excel worksheet. From this menu, you can also add additional toolbars to the window and add a header and/or footer to the workbook.

Insert Menu - The Insert menu is generally used for enhancing worksheets. From the Insert menu, you can insert graphics, charts, cells, hyperlinks, rows, columns, charts, and other Excel options.

Format Menu - The Format menu also contains a large number of worksheet-proofing tools. From this menu, you can format cells, rows, columns, and the worksheet. You can also access the AutoFormat, conditional formatting, and style options.

Tools Menu - The Tools menu contains several advanced manipulation tools, including spelling, worksheet protection, auditing, and macros.

Data Menu - The Data menu contains functions associated with organising and displaying worksheet data.

Window Menu - The Window menu allows you to create a new window with the same content, navigate between all open Excel workbooks, and arrange or split windows so that you can easily access any open workbook.

Help Menu - The Help menu can assist you with any questions you may have while creating a workbook. This menu also includes the Office Assistant, which you can use to answer questions.

Note - When you click a Menu bar option, a drop-down list will appear. This drop-down list contains the most commonly used features in that menu. You may want to expand the list to view all of the features. To do so, click the double arrows at the bottom of the drop-down list or double-click the name of the menu. The menu will expand to reveal its full functionality.

Standard Toolbar

The Standard toolbar allows you to manipulate a worksheet using shortcut buttons. Equipped with the most commonly used commands and operations, the Standard toolbar enables you to easily manage a worksheet.

The Standard toolbar is located directly below the Menu bar. You can hold the mouse cursor over each button to activate a screen tip containing the name of the button. The buttons that typically appear on the Standard toolbar are:

New - The New button opens a new, blank workbook. You can use this button instead of selecting **File > New**.

Open - The Open button opens an existing worksheet. You can use this button instead of selecting **File > Open**.

Save - The Save option saves over an existing file. If you click this button, you will not receive a prompt to save the file in another location.

Permission - The permission button provides access to Information Rights Management (IRM), which allows you to specify permission for access and use of documents or e-mail messages. This button helps prevent sensitive information from being printed, forwarded, or copied by unauthorised people.

E-Mail - The E-Mail option allows you to send an e-mail directly from an Excel workbook; you do not need to open the default e-mail application.

Print - The Print option automatically sends the file to the default printer.

Print Preview - This option allows you to view a full-page copy of the worksheet before you print it. Using this feature can reduce the need to reprint pages due to an alignment problem or other small, overlooked error.

Spelling and Grammar - This feature spell checks the worksheet and looks for grammatical errors. This feature will suggest alternate spellings and help reword sentences that contain grammatical errors.

Research - This button opens the **Research** task pane next to your worksheet. From this pane you can use the dictionary or thesaurus, search the Web, or even get translation services without leaving your workspace.

Cut - The Cut button allows you to remove any portion of text or graphics from the worksheet and place the item(s) in the system clipboard. The clipboard holds the item that you have removed until you decide to paste it into another area.

Copy - The Copy button is used to duplicate any portion of text, graphic, cell, row, or column in the worksheet. This button is very handy when you have a portion of text that needs to be repeated often or if you have a large range of cells that needs to be duplicated.

Paste - The Paste button works with the Copy and Cut buttons. After you have cut or copied an item, you can then paste that item anywhere in the worksheet.

Format Painter - The Format Painter allows you to use the format of one cell as a template for the format of other cells, rows, or columns in the worksheet.

Undo - The Undo option is a fail-safe feature built into all Microsoft Office products. The Undo feature allows you to undo whatever action just occurred.

Redo - The Redo button works alongside the Undo feature. If you accidentally used Undo, or "undid" too many actions, Redo will simply replace whatever action the Undo feature cancelled.

Insert Hyperlink - The Insert Hyperlink option allows you to create hyperlinks within the worksheet. These hyperlinks can link to a web page, another workbook, or even another cell within the worksheet.

AutoSum - AutoSum automatically creates a formula that adds together rows or columns of numerical information.

Sort Ascending - The Sort Ascending feature allows you to sort a selection of cells alphabetically from A to Z or numerically from the smallest number to the largest.

Sort Descending - The Sort Descending feature allows you to sort a selection of cells alphabetically from Z to A or numerically from the largest number to the smallest.

Chart Wizard - The Chart Wizard guides you through a four-step process to create a chart in the worksheet.

 Drawing - The Drawing button gives you quick access to the Drawing toolbar. The Drawing toolbar provides you with shortcuts to add and draw objects, format the colour of text and objects, and to a variety of other drawing features.

 Zoom - The Zoom feature allows you to view you worksheet at different sizes. The default is 100 percent.

Help - The Help option provides you with assistance while creating the worksheet.

Toolbar Options - The Toolbar Options button allows you to dock the toolbars in one or two rows, and add or remove buttons from the toolbar.

Although the Standard toolbar is typically found directly below the Menu bar, it is possible to move it, or any other toolbar, to a different location on the screen.

 If you are unable to view all the toolbar buttons, it is possible that the Formatting toolbar and the Standard toolbar may be combined on the same row. To move a toolbar, click and hold the line on the left edge of the toolbar and drag it further down the screen, or use the Show Buttons on Two Rows option from the Toolbar Options button.

Formatting Toolbar

The Formatting toolbar allows you to easily format the worksheet using shortcut buttons.

From left to right, the functions that typically appear on the Formatting toolbar are:

Font - The Font drop-down list allows you select which font you would like to use.

Font Size - The Font Size drop-down list allows you to select which text size you would like to use.

Bold - The Bold button allows you to bold highlighted text.

Italic - The Italic button allows you to italicize highlighted text.

Underline - The Underline button allows you to underline highlighted text.

Align Left - Align Left will align the text to the left side of a cell, row, column, or worksheet.

Align Center - Align Center will align the text in the center of any highlighted cell, row, column, or worksheet.

Align Right - Align Right will align the text to the right side of a cell, row, column, or worksheet.

Merge and Center - Merge and Center allows you to join together two or more cells. This option is helpful when you are creating a title heading.

Currency Style - The Currency Style button allows you to convert plain numbers into dollar amounts.

Percent Style - The Percent Style button converts plain numbers into percentages.

Comma Style - The Comma Style button will insert appropriate commas and a decimal point into plain numbers.

Increase Decimal - The Increase Decimal button allows you to add more decimal places to a numerical value.

Decrease Decimal - The Decrease Decimal button lessens the number of decimal places in a numerical value.

Decrease Indent - The Decrease Indent button will decrease the indentation of text by moving highlighted text to the left.

Increase Indent - The Increase Indent button will increase the indentation of text by moving highlighted text to the right.

Borders - You can divide the worksheet into visually appealing sections by placing a border around selected cells, rows or columns.

Fill Colour - Fill Colour colourises the background of a cell or group of cells.

Font Colour - The Font Colour button changes the font colour of highlighted cells.

Toolbar Options - The Toolbar Options button allows you to dock the toolbars in one or two rows, and add or remove buttons from the toolbar.

Cells, Rows, Columns and Worksheets

A worksheet is a collection of rows and columns that are displayed on-screen in a scrollable window. The intersection of each row and column is called a cell. A cell can hold a number, a text string, or a formula.

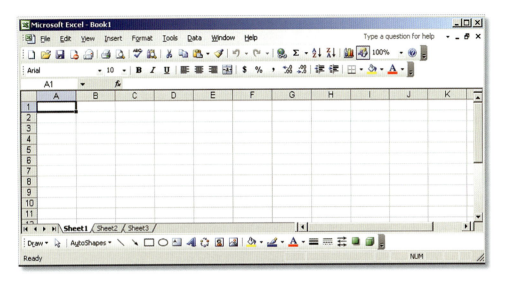

Cell
A cell is the most basic part of a spreadsheet. The cell name starts with the column and ends with the row, for example, A1.

Rows
A row is a horizontal line or group of cells. Rows are numbered from one to 65,536.

Columns
A column is a vertical line or group of cells. There can be up to 256 columns in a spreadsheet.

Worksheet/Spreadsheet
A worksheet, also called a spreadsheet, is the basic document that stores all imputed data. A worksheet is comprised of rows, columns, and cells.

The Name Box and Formula Bar

The Name box is located below the Formatting toolbar on the left side of the screen. The Name box displays the name of the cell that is currently active. You can also view a defined range of cells by clicking the down arrow to the right of the Name box and selecting the range.

The Formula bar displays the entire contents of the cell, including cell value, text, and formulas. The Formula bar is best utilised when editing cell information.

Sheet Tabs and Scrollbars

Workbooks will often contain many individual worksheets. You may change the name of each sheet tab to correspond with the topic you are covering in the worksheet. You will also create worksheets that are larger than the viewing area on the computer screen. Familiarising yourself with the scrollbars will enable you to view more of the worksheet with just a click of the mouse.

Sheet Tabs - Sheet tabs are located at the bottom of the worksheet. Each tab represents a separate worksheet. The default names of the sheet tabs are Sheet1, Sheet2, and Sheet3. Sheet tab names can have up to 31 characters.

Sheet Tab Scroll Buttons - Sheet tab scroll buttons are located in the bottom left corner of the worksheet. These buttons let you easily navigate to other worksheets in the workbook. Sheet tab scroll buttons are especially handy when the workbook contains many worksheets and you are unable to view all the sheet tabs.

To move one sheet forward or backward, click the button with a single triangle facing forward or backward, respectively. To skip to the first or last sheet tab, click the appropriate button with a single triangle pointing to a line.

Scrollbars - Scrollbars are located vertically on the right side of the worksheet and horizontally in the bottom right corner of the worksheet. Scrollbars allow you to see the parts of the worksheet that go beyond the regular viewing area.

Using the Office Assistant

The Office Assistant is an animation that helps you retrieve information on any of the features in Excel.

To show and use the Office Assistant:

Step 1: From the **Help** menu, select **Show the Office Assistant.**

Step 2: Click the Office Assistant icon.

Step 3: In the **What would you like to do?** text field, enter a question and click **Search**.

To hide the Office Assistant:

From the **Help** menu, select **Hide the Office Assistant**, or right-click the **Office Assistant**, and select **Hide** from the pop-up menu.

To change the appearance of the Office Assistant:

Step 1: Make the Office Assistant visible.

Step 2: Right-click the **Office Assistant**, and select **Choose Assistant**... from the pop-up menu.

Step 3: In the dialog box, click the **Next** button until you find an Office Assistant that you like.

Step 4: Click **OK**.

To get help at any time, make sure the Office Assistant is visible, and then click the Office Assistant. Enter a question in the box that appears. Click **Search**. The Office Assistant runs a search and provides a list of related topics. If you would like to view a topic, simply click it. If the requested topic is not listed, you may try searching again with different key words or search for the topic on the Internet.

Note - When completing certain operations, a light bulb will appear beside the Office Assistant. If you click the bulb, the Office Assistant will provide you with some useful tips relating to the current operation.

Summary

The key points discussed in this lesson are:

◆ Identifying and using the features found on the Title bar, Menu bar, and Standard and Formatting toolbars.

◆ The features found on the Standard and Formatting toolbar can replace the multi-step features located in the Menu bar.

◆ The definition of a cell, row, column, and worksheet.

◆ Using the Name box and Formula bar to more easily identify cell names, range names, and the complete contents of a cell.

◆ Navigating through the Excel application window by using scrollbars and sheet tabs.

◆ Using the Office Assistant to find the answers to any questions you might have while creating a workbook and how to format the Office Assistant to your own specifications.

Opening and Creating a Workbook

When getting started with Excel it can be helpful to first view an existing workbook or a custom template. You are going to learn how to complete both of these operations as well as learn how to create your own workbook from a blank document.

Objectives

Upon completing this module, you will be able to:

✔ Open an existing Excel workbook

✔ Open an existing template

✔ Create a new Excel workbook

✔ Save your own custom template

Opening an Existing Excel Workbook

Often, you will need to access an existing workbook that someone else created. To do so, you will need to know the name and location of the file.

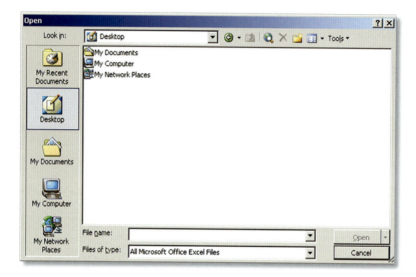

To open an existing workbook:

From the **File** menu, select **Open**. An Open dialog box appears.
In the **Look in**: field, navigate to the folder where the workbook is located.
Click the workbook you want to open, and click **Open**.

Opening a Custom Template

Creating a template allows you to preset specific formats and formulas in a workbook. Templates can save time and ensure consistency when developing documents for specific topics or customers. A good example of a template is an expense report. Other individuals can use the same template, so this will ensure that they use the proper procedures and formulate accurate calculations.

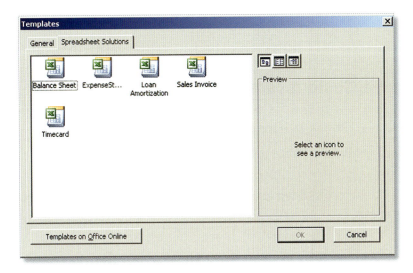

To open an existing template:

Step 1: From the **File** menu, select **New**. The New **Workspace** task pane will open next to the right side of your workbook.

Step 2: Select the **On my computer**... option. The Templates dialog box will open.

Step 3: In the Templates dialog box, there are two tabs: **General** and **Spreadsheet Solutions.** Click either tab to view template options.

Step 4: You can select the Workbook option for a blank workbook, or you may select a template that suits your needs. In most cases, you can click a template and preview the template in the Preview window.

Step 5: Click the template you would like to use, and click **OK**.

Creating a New Workbook

Creating a new workbook allows you to display and organise data both in text and graphical formats.

To open a new workbook:

Step 1: From the File menu, select New.

Step 2: In the New Workspace task pane, click the Blank workbook option.

Saving a Custom Template

To save a workbook as a template:

Step 1: From the **File** menu, select **Save As**. A Save As dialog box opens.

Step 2: From the **Save as type:** field, use the down arrow to select **Template.**

Step 3: In the **File Name**: field, enter the title of the template.

Step 4: In the **Save In**: field, select the location where you want to save the workbook. Click **Save**.

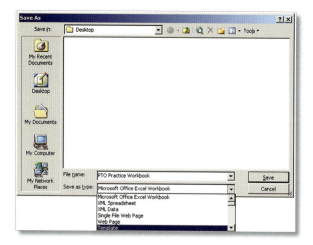

Summary

The key points discussed in this lesson are:

◆ Opening an existing Excel workbook.

◆ Opening a custom template.

◆ Creating a new workbook.

◆ Saving a custom template.

Entering and Formatting Text

Creating worksheets in Excel is not limited to inputting numbers and text. Excel also allows you to manipulate data visually and draw attention to key parts of the worksheet. Formatting text or adding colour to cells can be as impacting as the information itself. Making your worksheets visually appealing and informative can transform what might seem unexciting into something powerful and appealing. You are going to learn time-saving shortcuts to format a worksheet.

Objectives

Upon completing this lesson, you will be able to:

- ✔ Enter and edit text
- ✔ Resize rows and columns
- ✔ Merge cells
- ✔ Format the worksheet manually
- ✔ Create hyperlinks
- ✔ Use AutoFormat
- ✔ Rotate text and change indents
- ✔ Use AutoFill
- ✔ Define styles
- ✔ Apply number formats
- ✔ Format cells

Entering and Editing Text

The two basic types of data used in a worksheet are values and formulas. Values consist of numbers and text. A formula is a calculation based on information contained in specific cells. You will learn to create formulas in a later module.

To add text to a cell:

Step 1: Click any cell.

Step 2: Enter text, and press Enter.

To edit the text within a cell:

Step 1: Click the cell that you want to edit.

Step 2: Enter new text over the old text, and press **Enter**.

OR

Step 1: Double-click the cell that you want to edit.

Step 2: A cursor will appear inside the cell. You can partially or completely delete the contents of the cell by highlighting the text that you want to delete and pressing Backspace.

Step 3: Retype the text, and press **Enter**.

Resizing Rows and Columns

Occasionally, a column or row is not large enough to hold the text that you wish to enter. There are several ways to resize rows and columns so that all of the text is visible.

To increase/decrease row height:

Step 1: Place the mouse on the bottom border of the row heading whose height needs to be increased or decreased. The cursor will change into a black plus sign with arrows on each end of the vertical line.

Step 2: Click and drag the mouse so that the row is the desired height. Release the mouse.

To increase/decrease column width:

Step 1: Place the mouse on the right border of the column heading whose width needs to be increased or decreased. The cursor will change into a black plus sign with arrows on each end of the horizontal line.

Step 2: Click and drag the mouse so that the column is the desired width. Release the mouse.

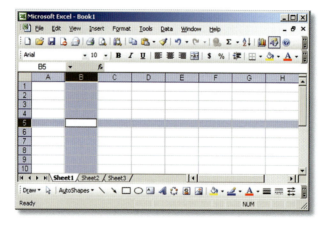

To resize rows using the Format menu:

Step 1: Select the rows you want to resize.

Step 2: From the **Format** menu, select **Row**. A drop-down list will appear.

Step 3: Select either **Autofit** or **Height**. If you select **Autofit**, Excel will individually adjust the selected rows to fit the text precisely. If you select **Height**, the Row Height dialog box will open and ask you to enter the row height.

Step 4: Enter the row height, and click **OK**.

To resize columns using the Format menu:

Step 1: Select the columns you want to resize.

Step 2: From the **Format** menu, select **Column**. A drop-down list will appear.

Step 3: Select either **Autofit** or **Width**. If you select Autofit, Excel will individually adjust the selected columns to fit the text precisely. If you select **Width**, the Column Width dialog box will open and ask you to enter the column width.

Step 4: Enter the column width, and click **OK**.

Formatting Cell Properties

This section covers how to vertically align text inside of a cell and how to wrap text so that each cell grows automatically as you type. This feature keeps you from continually resizing rows and columns to accommodate the contents of the cells.

To vertically align the contents of the cells:

Step 1: Select the cells you want to format. (You can select the entire worksheet by clicking the empty cell that falls between Row Heading 1 and Column Heading A. The entire worksheet will highlight.)

Step 2: From the **Format** menu, select **Cells**.... The Format Cells dialog box will appear. Click the **Alignment** tab.

Step 3: In the **Text alignment section**, click the down arrow next to the **Vertical**: field.

Step 4: From the pop-up list, choose how you would like the text to vertically align, and click **OK**.

To apply text wrap to the contents of the cells:

Step 1: Select the cells you want to format.

Step 2: From the **Format** menu, select **Cells**.... The Format Cells dialog box will appear. Click the **Alignment** tab.

Step 3: In the Text control section, click the checkbox next to Wrap text. Click **OK**.

Note - To see how Text Wrap works, type into any cell in your Practice worksheet. When the text exceeds the width of the cell, follow the steps listed above and notice how the text will "wrap", causing the row that the cell is in to adjust in height.

Merging Cells

Merging the data contained in one cell with blank, adjacent cells is useful when creating a decorative title for the worksheet.

To create a title with merged cells:

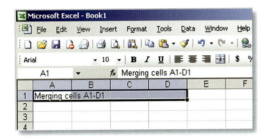

Step 1: Enter the title in the upper-left cell of the range that will be merged, and press **Enter**.

Step 2: Select the range of cells in which the title is to be placed.

Step 3: On the Formatting toolbar, click the **Merge and Center** button.

Formatting the Worksheet

You can create a worksheet suited to your own personal tastes and objectives, and draw attention to parts of the worksheet that you would like to highlight, by using formats like bold, italics, and underline.

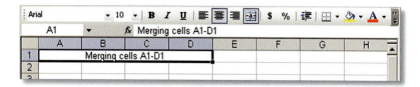

To format the text using the Formatting toolbar:

Step 1: Click the cell you want to format. This selects all of the text within the cell. To select only part of the text within the cell, double-click the cell and then highlight the text you want to format.

Step 2: Using the Formatting toolbar, click:

B **B** to bold the text.

I **I** to italicise the text.

U **U** to underline the text.

≡ The **Align Left** button to align the text flush with the left side of the cell.

≡ The **Align Center** button to align the text in the center of the cell.

≡ The **Align Right** button to align the text flush with the right side of the cell.

To use the Format Painter:

Step 1: Select a cell or range that has the formatting you want to copy.

Step 2: On the Standard toolbar, click the **Format Painter** button.

Step 3: Click the cells to which you want to apply the format.

 Note - If you want to apply a format to non-contiguous cells, double-click the Format Painter button instead of single-clicking it. When you finish copying the formatting to destination cells, click the Format Painter button again or press Escape to de-select it.

Creating Hyperlinks

You can create internal hyperlinks that link a cell on one worksheet to a cell on another worksheet. You can also create external hyperlinks that will launch a webpage or even another software application.

To create an internal hyperlink:

Step 1: Click the cell you want to attach a link to.

Step 2: On the Standard toolbar, click the **Insert Hyperlink** button. The Insert Hyperlink dialog box appears.

Step 3: In the **Link to:** area, select **Existing File or Webpage.**

Step 4: There are several ways of entering the hyperlink information. In the **Look in:** section, you can choose to search three different areas: **Current Folder, Browsed Pages,** or **Recent Files**.

OR

In the **Address:** section, you can manually type a Web page address. For example, enter this Web page address in the **Address:** section: www.office.Microsoft.com. Click **OK**.

Step 5: To test the hyperlink, click the hyperlink to open a browser window and view www.office.Microsoft.com.

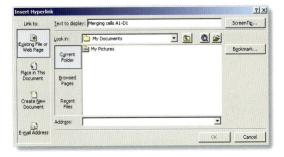

You have just created an internal link that hyperlinks a cell on one worksheet to a cell on another worksheet. Click the hyperlink to test it.

To create an external hyperlink:

Step 1: Click the cell you wish to attach a link to: select any cell on the Practice worksheet.

Step 2: On the Standard toolbar, click the **Insert Hyperlink** button. The Insert Hyperlink dialog box appears.

Step 3: In the **Link to:** area, select **Existing File or Webpage.**

Step 4: There are several ways of entering the hyperlink information. In the **Look in:** section, you can choose to search three different areas: **Current Folder, Browsed Pages,** or **Recent Files**.

OR

In the **Address:** section, you can manually type a Web page address. For example, enter this Web page address in the **Address:** section: www.office.Microsoft.com. Click **OK**.

Step 5: To test the hyperlink, click the hyperlink to open a browser window and view www.office.Microsoft.com.

Rotating Text and Changing Indents

Rotating text within a cell can create interesting visual effects, drawing attention to key parts of the worksheet.

To rotate the text within a cell(s):

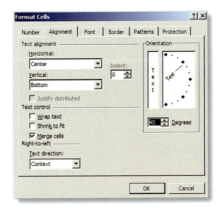

Step 1: Select the cells you wish to rotate.

Step 2: From the **Format** menu, select **Cells**.... The Format Cells dialog box will appear. Click the **Alignment** tab.

Step 3: In the **Orientation** section, click in the half-circle to set a rotation angle. Click **OK**.

When data is entered into a cell, text is automatically aligned to the left side of the cell and numbers to the right side.

To indent text in a cell

Step 1: Select the cells you want to indent.

Step 2: On the Formatting toolbar, click **Increase Indent.**

Step 3: To decrease or remove indentation, click **Decrease Indent.**

Using AutoFill

Using AutoFill, you can automatically continue a series of numbers, text/number combinations, or dates, based on a pattern you establish. For example: 1,2,3,4 or January, February, March or Monday, Tuesday, Wednesday. This can be achieved by using the Fill Handle. The Fill Handle is a black square located in the lower right corner of the selected cell.

To use AutoFill:

Step 1: To generate month names in a range of cells, enter "January" into cell A1.

Step 2: Point to the fill handle with the mouse; the mouse pointer changes to a black fill handle (looks like a black plus sign).

Step 3: Click and drag from cell A1 to cell A12, and then release the mouse button.

Defining Styles

Defining styles allows you to preset cell format, making it easy to apply a specific style to an entire group of cells or worksheet. Styles that you can choose from include: Number, Alignment, Font, Border, Patterns, and Protection.

To define a style:

Step 1: Select the cell.

Step 2: From the **Format** menu, select **Style**.

Step 3: In the **Style includes** section, a check mark appears in each of the format types. To deselect formatting from the cell, click the box to clear the check mark.

Step 4: In the Style dialog box, the **Style name:** field will read Normal. Double-click the text and enter a new name for the style. The new name could reflect the visual aspects of the style, i.e. Red text on black, or the meaning of the cell, i.e. Worksheet headers. Click **OK**.

To delete a style:

Step 1: From the **Format** menu, select **Style**. The Style dialog box appears.

Step 2: From the **Style name:** drop-down box, select the style you would like to delete.

Step 3: Click the **Delete** button, and click **OK**.

Using AutoFormatting

AutoFormats are professionally designed colour and formatting schemes.

To apply an AutoFormat:

Step 1: Select a range of cells.

Step 2: From the **Format** menu, select **AutoFormat**.... The AutoFormat dialog box appears.

Step 3: Using the scroll bars inside the AutoFormat dialog box, view the different formats.

Step 4: Click the format that you would like to use. Click **OK**.

Applying Number Formats

By applying number formats, you can enter regular numeric values and format them into monetary values, dates, fractions, etc.

To apply number formats:

Step 1: Select the cells you wish to format.

Step 2: From the **Format** menu, select **Cells**.... The Format Cells dialog box will appear.

Step 3: Click the **Number** tab. The **Category:** section contains a variety of number formats.

Step 4: Click each option to view a sample of how the text will look. Click the desired option and then click **OK**.

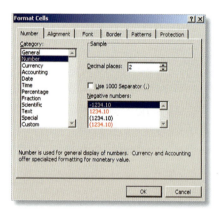

Note - Most of the selections will have additional options from which you can choose. For example, if you select Currency as the number format, you can then select how many decimal places you wish the number to represent, what pound sign symbol you wish to use, and how you want to see negative numbers displayed.

Formatting Cell Borders

Placing a border around cells can visually enhance the worksheet and separate key information for easier understanding.

To apply borders:

Step 1: Select the cells to add borders.

Step 2: On the Formatting toolbar, click the drop-down arrow to the right of the **Borders** button.

Step 3: Click the desired border.

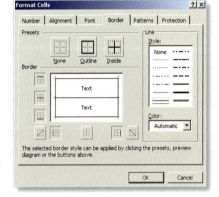

To format borders:

Step 1: Select the cells whose borders you wish to format.

Step 2: From the **Format** menu, select **Cells**.... The Format Cells dialog box appears.

Step 3: Click the **Borders** tab. Within the dialog box are several options for Presets and Borders:

Preset Options	Border Options	
None - no visible border	Top of the cell	Left side of cell
Outline - heavy outline	Between cells	None/Empty
Inside - mimics gridlines, but only for selected cells	Bottom of the cell	Right side of cell
	Diagonal (forward)	Diagonal (backwards)

Step 4: To change the line style of the cell borders, click the line style you would like, and then click the border you wish to change.

Step 5: To change the colour of the border, click the drop-down arrow in the **Colour:** selection area. Click the colour of choice, and then click the borders to which you would like to apply the colour. Click **OK**.

Applying Cell Shading

Adding colour to cells can help separate ideas, statistics, key points, and other specialised information.

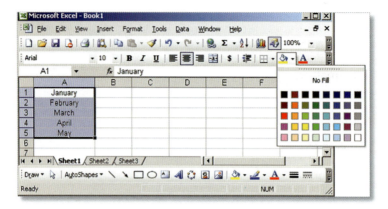

To apply colour shading to a cell or group of cells:

Step 1: Select the cell(s) to which you would like to add colour/shading.

Step 2: On the Formatting toolbar, click the **Fill Colour** arrow. A drop-down list of colours will appear.

Step 3: Click the colour you would like to add.

Summary

The key points discussed in this lesson are:

- Creating your own stylised workbook by entering and editing text.
- Creating rows and columns that are sized to appropriately fit the text in worksheets.
- Formatting cell properties so that the text fits inside each cell automatically without having to manually adjust each row or column.
- Creating a heading for the worksheet by merging cells together.
- Formatting the parts of the worksheet: text, cell, row, and column so that the data is displayed in a visually appealing and functional format.
- Creating hyperlinks to other places in the workbook, other applications, and web pages.
- Rotating text and changing indents in cells so that the information is displayed properly.
- Using AutoFill to automatically continue a series of numbers, text/number combinations, or dates, based on a pattern you establish.
- Defining Styles so that you can preset how the cells will look, making it easy to apply a specific style to an entire group of cells or worksheet.
- Applying number formats, you can enter regular numeric values and format them into monetary values, dates, fractions, etc.
- Formatting a border around the cells in the worksheet can visually enhance and separate key information for easier understanding.
- Applying shading to the cells can help separate ideas, statistics, key points, and other specialised information.

Managing Cells, Rows, Columns and Worksheets

Managing a worksheet is key to creating a valuable, ever-changing document. You are going to learn the basic tools needed to manage cells, rows, columns, and worksheets.

Objectives

Upon completing this lesson, you will be able to:

✔ Insert, delete, copy, and clear cells, rows, columns, and worksheets

✔ Use drag and drop to copy cells

✔ Hide and un-hide rows and columns

✔ Freeze and unfreeze rows and columns

✔ Use Find and Replace

Inserting Cells, Rows, Columns and Worksheets

As you create a workbook, you will often need to add a cell, row, column or entire worksheet.

To insert a cell:

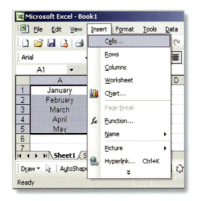

Step 1: Select the cell(s) below or to the right of where the new cell is to be inserted.

Step 2: From the **Insert** menu, select **Cells**…. Depending on the cells you selected, Excel will ask you if you want to shift the cells down or to the right, or if you want to insert an entire row or column. Select the option that you want and then click **OK**.

To insert a row or column:

Step 1: Select the row header below where the new row will be inserted.
OR
Step 1: Select the column header to the right of where the new column is to be inserted.

Step 2: From the **Insert** menu, select either **Rows** or **Columns**, depending on which you want to insert.

To insert multiple rows or columns:

Step 1: Click and drag over the amount of rows or columns equal to the number you want to insert.

Step 2: From the **Insert** menu, select **Rows** or **Columns**.

Note - A row or column can also be inserted by right-clicking the row number or column header and then selecting **Insert** from the pop-up menu.

To insert a worksheet:

From the **Insert** menu, select **Worksheet**. A worksheet will appear in the workbook.

To move a worksheet:

Step 1: Click and hold the sheet tab of the worksheet you would like to move. The cursor will look like an arrow with a piece of paper attached to it.

Step 2: As you move the mouse, a small, upside down, black triangle will appear between each of the other worksheets. This indicates where the new worksheet will be moved to when you release the mouse button. Decide where you want the new worksheet and then release the mouse button.

Deleting Cells, Rows, Columns and Worksheets

Deleting cells, rows and columns follows the same general guidelines as inserting cells, rows and columns.

When cells are deleted, a dialog box appears that asks if you would like to shift the remaining cells up, down, to the right or left. When rows are deleted, the rows below the deleted row(s) move up to fill the space. When columns are deleted, the columns to the right of the deleted column(s) shift to the left.

To delete a cell:

Step 1: Click the cell(s) you wish to delete.

Step 2: From the **Edit** menu, select **Delete**.

Step 3: From the Delete dialog box, select whether you want the remaining cells to shift up or to the left or if you want to delete the entire row or column. (If you are deleting more than one cell, based on the selection, Excel will automatically suggest which way to shift the remaining cells. You can change the selection by clicking the radio button next to your choice.)

To delete a row(s) or column(s):

Step 1: Click the row number(s) or column header(s) of the row or column to be deleted.

Step 2: From the **Edit** menu, select **Delete**.

To delete a worksheet:

Step 1: Make sure that you are viewing the worksheet that you want to delete. From the **Edit** menu, select **Delete Sheet**. The Microsoft Excel dialog box will appear.

Step 2: The dialog box will instruct you to click **OK** if you are sure you want to permanently delete the sheet, or to click **Cancel** if you do not want to delete the worksheet. Click **OK** or **Cancel**.

 Note - Once you delete a worksheet, it is permanently gone. You cannot undo a deleted worksheet.

Copying Cells, Rows, Columns and Worksheets

You can use the **Copy** and **Paste** functions to repeat the same data multiple times, without having to re-enter the information.

To copy a cell:

Step 1: Select the cell you wish to copy.

Step 2: From the Standard toolbar, click the **Copy** button.

Step 3: Click the destination cell.

Step 4: From the Standard toolbar, click the Paste button.

There are several ways to copy and paste rows and columns. Each way creates a different end result.

To copy a row(s) and insert it as an additional row into a worksheet:

Step 1: Select the row(s) you wish to copy.

Step 2: From the Standard toolbar, click the **Copy** button.

Step 3: Click the row header below where you want the copied row(s) to be inserted.

Step 4: From the **Insert** menu, select **Copied Cells**.

 Note - Although you are selecting **Copied Cells**, the worksheet will actually insert the copied rows. If you were to select Paste, the copied rows would overwrite, rather than insert, information in the worksheet.

To copy a row(s) and insert it over an existing row in the worksheet:

Step 1: Select the row(s) you wish to copy.

Step 2: From the Standard toolbar, click the **Copy** button.

Step 3: Click on the row number of the row(s) you want to overwrite.

Step 4: From the Standard toolbar, click **Paste**.

 Note - You will notice that the rows you just inserted into the worksheet replace/overwrite the rows that previously existed there. So, you will want to be careful when copying and pasting rows into the worksheet that you follow the correct procedure. Remember: you can always click the **Undo** button on the **Standard** toolbar if you accidentally insert rows incorrectly.

To copy a column(s) and insert it as an additional column into the worksheet:

Step 1: To copy a column(s) and insert it as an additional column into the worksheet:

Step 2: Select the column(s) you wish to copy.

Step 3: From the Standard toolbar, click the **Copy** button.

Step 4: Click the column header to the right of where you want the copied column(s) to be inserted.

Step 5: From the **Insert** menu, select **Copied Cells**.

 Note - Inserting copied columns follows the same procedure for inserting copied rows.

To copy a column(s) and insert it over an existing column in the worksheet:

Step 1: Select the column(s) you wish to copy.

Step 2: From the Standard toolbar, click the **Copy** button.

Step 3: Click the column header of the column you want to overwrite.

Step 4: From the **Standard** toolbar, click **Paste**.

 Note - Using this method overwrites the columns where the inserted columns now reside.

To copy a worksheet:

Step 1: Make sure you are viewing the worksheet to be copied.

Step 2: From the **Edit** menu, select **Move or Copy Sheet**. The Move or Copy dialog box will open.

Step 3: In the **Before sheet:** section, click on the title of the worksheet before which you would like the copied sheet to be inserted. Keep in mind that the copied worksheet will be inserted before the worksheet you select.

Step 4: Click the box next to **Create a copy**. Click **OK**.

To move a worksheet to a new workbook:

Step 1: Make sure you are viewing the worksheet you wish to move.

Step 2: From the **Edit** menu, select **Move or Copy Sheet**. The Move or Copy dialog box will open.

Step 3: In the **To book:** section, from the drop-down arrow, select **(new book)**. This will open a new workbook for you.

Using Drag and Drop

An easy way to copy cells is to drag and drop the data.

To copy cells using drag and drop:

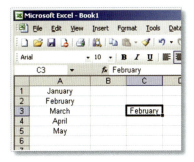

Step 1: Select the cells to be copied, and hold down the **Ctrl** key.

Step 2: When you place the cursor just slightly above the bottom right corner of the selected cells it will turn into a white pointer arrow with a small, black plus sign in the upper-right corner.

Step 3: Once you see the change in the cursor, drag the selected cell(s) to the destination cell(s).

Step 4: Release the mouse to copy the data into the new location.

To copy cells to a different sheet using drag and drop:

Step 1: Select the cells to be copied, and hold down the **Ctrl** and **Alt** keys.

Step 2: Using the same cursor as before, drag the selected cell(s) to the sheet tab of the destination worksheet. Excel automatically switches to that sheet.

Step 3: To drop the data into the new location, release the mouse over the destination cells.

Clearing Cell, Row and Column Content

When cells, rows and columns are deleted, they are removed from the worksheet entirely. But when a cell, row or column is cleared, they remain in the worksheet, while only the content or format is cleared.

To clear the content from a cell, row or column:

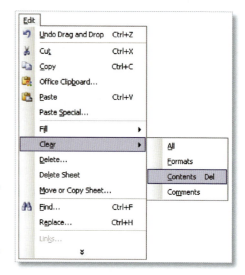

Step 1: Select the cell(s), row(s), or column(s) whose content you wish to clear.

Step 2: From the **Edit** menu, select **Clear** and then from the drop-down list, select **Contents Del**.

To clear the format from a cell, row or column:

Step 1: Select the cell(s), row(s), or column(s) whose format you wish to clear.

Step 2: From the **Edit** menu, select **Clear** and then from the drop-down list, select **Formats**.

To clear the content and formatting from a cell, row or column:

Step 1: Select the cell(s), row(s), or column(s) you wish to clear entirely.

Step 2: From the **Edit** menu, select **Clear** and then from the drop-down list, select **All**.

Hiding and Un-Hiding Rows and Columns

Excel enables you to hide rows and columns in the worksheet without losing any of the hidden information.

To hide a single row or column:

Step 1: Right-click the row number or column header that you wish to hide.

Step 2: From the **Shortcut** menu, select **Hide**.

To hide multiple rows or columns:

Step 1: Select the rows or columns you wish to hide.

Step 2: Right-click one of the selected rows or columns.

Step 3: From the **Shortcut** menu, select **Hide**.

To unhide rows or columns:

Step 1: Select the rows or columns on both sides of the hidden row(s) or column(s).

Step 2: Right-click the selection and from the **Shortcut** menu, select **Unhide**.

 Note - If you hide Column A or Row 1, to unhide you must use the mouse to resize the column or row. Following the same instructions you used earlier to resize columns and rows, place the mouse to the left side of column B or the top side of Row 2. When the cursor turns into the sizing cursor, click and drag to reopen/unhide Column A or Row 1.

Freezing and Unfreezing Rows and Columns

If you want the column headers to be visible as you scroll through the data, you can freeze that portion of the worksheet.

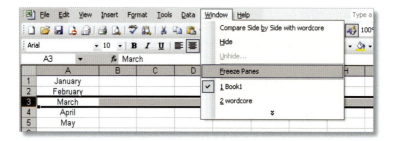

To freeze a row:

Step 1: Select the row below where you want the split to appear.

Step 2: From the **Window** menu, select **Freeze Panes**.

To unfreeze a row or column:

From the **Window** menu, select **Unfreeze Panes**.

To freeze a column:

Step 1: Select the column to the right of where you want the split to appear.

Step 2: From the **Window** menu, select **Freeze Panes**.

To freeze both a row and a column:

Step 1: Click the cell below and to the right of where you want the split to appear.

Step 2: From the **Window** menu, select **Freeze Panes**.

Using Find and Replace

A very convenient feature of Excel is Find and Replace. Find and Replace allows you to find a specific word in the worksheet and replace it with another.

To use Find and Replace:

Step 1: From the **Edit** menu, select **Replace**.

Step 2: In the **Find what:** field, type the word you are searching for.

Step 3: In the **Replace with:** field, type in the word you want to replace the "find" word with.

Step 4: In the **Search:** field drop-down list, select if you would like to search the worksheet by rows or columns.

Step 5: Click the **Find Next** button.

Step 6: Excel will search the worksheet for the "find what" word.

Step 7: When Excel locates the word, you have several options:

• Click the **Replace** button if you want to replace it with the "replace" word.

• Click the **Replace All** button if you want to replace all instances of the "find" word in the worksheet.

OR

• Click the **Find Next** button to skip to the next instance of the word without replacing it.

Step 8: Click **Close** when you are finished.

Summary

The key points discussed in this lesson are:

◆ Inserting cells, rows, columns and worksheets so that the workbook can grow larger as you acquire additional data as well as how to delete cells, rows, columns, and worksheets so that you can remove unwanted information from the workbook.

◆ Using the Copy and Paste functions to repeat the same data multiple times, without having to re-enter the information, as well as how to use Drag and Drop as an easy method of copying information from cell to cell.

◆ Clearing a cell, row or column so that it remains in the worksheet, clearing only the content or format. And how to hide and unhide rows and columns in the worksheet so that only the information you want to be seen is visible to other people.

◆ Freezing and unfreezing column and row headers so that they are always visible as you scroll through the data.

◆ Using Find and Replace to find a specific word in the worksheet and replace it with another.

Module 2: Enhancing the Workbook

Excel not only provides the tools needed to create powerful worksheets that perform basic and advanced mathematical calculations, but also provides the flexibility to add impact to workbooks by adding charts, Clip Art, and objects. In this module, you will learn how to create formulas, add valuable visual aids, and properly set up pages in order for worksheets to print correctly.

Objectives

Upon completing this module, you will be able to:

- Identify the components of a formula
- Create and edit formulas
- Use AutoSum
- Create functions
- Link worksheets and consolidate data
- Create and format a chart
- Insert, edit, move, and delete Clip Art
- Use the Drawing toolbar to create and modify objects
- Save a workbook
- Send a workbook via e-mail
- Set up and preview a workbook
- Print a worksheet

Outline

This module contains these lessons:

- Working with Formulas
- Basic Functions and References
- Creating Charts
- Adding Clip Art
- Inserting and Formatting Objects
- Saving The Workbook
- Setting Up The Workbook
- Printing The Workbook

Working with Formulas

Excel formulas can be used to perform simple calculations like addition, subtraction, multiplication, and division, as well as complex calculations. Using formulas allows you to manage and display important information in a concise, concrete way.

Objectives

Upon completing this lesson, you will be able to:

- ✔ Identify a formula
- ✔ Identify operator symbols
- ✔ Create a formula
- ✔ Use AutoSum
- ✔ Edit formulas

What is a Formula?

Formulas usually consist of one or more cell addresses or values and a mathematical operator, such as +, -, * and /. For example, the following formula adds together the values found in cells B8 and G8:

=B8+G8

There are three types of formulas:

Text formula - Uses text and may contain the text operator ampersand (&) that joins (concatenates) two numbers. For example, typing =123&456 in a cell displays 123456 in that cell.

Numeric formula - Contains arithmetic operators like +, -, *, /, ^, and %. For example, =(A1+A2+A3+A4) or =(A1:A4)

Logical formula - Contains comparison operators like >, <, <=, >= and <>.

Note - A formula can be up to 255 characters long, and must begin with an equal sign (=). Formulas do not accept spaces, except between sets of letters, numbers, or symbols enclosed in quotation marks.

What is an Operator?

An operator identifies the calculation being performed by the formula. Operators available in Excel are:

• Addition +	• Greater Than >
• Subtraction -	• Less Than <
• Multiplication *	• Greater Than or Equal To >=
• Division /	• Less Than or Equal To <=
• Exponential ^	• Not Equal To <>
• Equal to =	• Concatenation &

Entering a Formula

There are several ways to enter formulas. You can enter a formula directly into a cell or you can use the Formula bar.

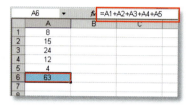

To add a formula using the point and click method:

Step 1: Click in the cell where the formula will reside.

Step 2: Type =.

Step 3: Click the cell whose address appears first in the formula. For example, to add cells A3 and A4, click A3.

Step 4: Type the mathematical operator after the value to indicate the next operation to be performed. For example, + (plus sign) to add.

Step 5: Continue to add cells to the formula, if any exist. Remember to type the operators between each cell that you add to the formula.

Step 6: Press **Enter**.

To add a formula manually in a cell:

Step 1: Click in the cell where the formula is to reside.

Step 2: Type =.

Step 3: Type the name of the cell whose address is first in the formula.

Step 4: Type the mathematical operator after the value to indicate the next operation to be performed.

Step 5: Continue to add cells to the formula. Remember to type the operators between each cell that you add to the formula.

Step 6: Press **Enter**.

Using AutoSum

AutoSum automatically builds a SUM formula based on a contiguous range of numbers.

To AutoSum rows or columns:

Step 1: Select the range of cells to be totalled.

Step 2: On the Standard toolbar, click the **AutoSum** button. The cell below the selected range shows the total/AutoSum.

Editing Formulas

As you build, change, and add information to worksheets, you may need to edit formulas already in place.

To edit a formula:

Click in the cell containing the formula to be edited. Notice the formula also appears in the formula bar.

Working in the formula bar, highlight the text that needs to be edited and retype the correct information. Make sure to include the operators as you edit the formula.

Press **Enter** when you are finished.

Note - If you are only adding cells to the formula, you can use the point and click method by clicking directly on the cells that you want to add to the formula. The cell names will appear in the formula bar as you click them.

Summary

The key points discussed in this lesson are:

◆ Formulas usually consist of one or more cell addresses or values and a mathematical operator, such as +, -, * and /.

◆ An Operator identifies the calculation being performed by a formula.

◆ Entering a formula directly into a cell or using the Formula bar, as well as how to use the AutoSum tool.

Basic Functions and References

A function is a built-in formula that performs calculations based on predetermined rules. There are hundreds of built-in functions in Excel. Knowing how to use functions can reduce the amount of time you spend tabulating a worksheet.

Objectives

Upon completing this lesson, you will be able to:

- ✔ Enter functions using the Formula Palette
- ✔ Use references
- ✔ Use date functions
- ✔ Use financial functions
- ✔ Use logical functions
- ✔ Link worksheets and consolidate data using 3-D references

What is a Function?

A function is a predefined formula that performs calculations by using specific values, called arguments, in a particular order. For example, the SUM function adds values in a selected range.

When do you use a function?

You would use a function to simplify and shorten formulas in a worksheet. For example, instead of using the formula =A1+A2+A3+A4 you can use the function =SUM(A1:A4).

Specifying Arguments

In order to perform certain tasks, functions require specific information called arguments. Arguments are values that are passed to the functions to perform operations. The number of arguments in a function varies between 0 and 14 and the length is restricted to 255 characters, including quotation marks, if any. Arguments can be constants, cells or ranges, range names, or functions.

Structure of a function

Remember the following when creating a function:

- A function begins with =.
- Then the function name, for example, SUM, ROUND, IF, FV.
- The function name is followed by ((open parenthesis).
- Then the arguments for the function separated by commas, for example, A2:A5,B2:B5.
- Then a) (close parenthesis) finishes the function.

Basic Functions

Some of the commonly used functions and their purposes are listed below:

AVERAGE - Averages the values in a selected range

CONCATENATE - Joins cell values together in a single cell

COUNT - Counts the number of cells that contain numbers within the list of arguments

IF - Displays a value that depends on the set criteria

LEFT and **RIGHT** - Returns a specific number of characters from the left (or right) end of a cell's value

MAX - Finds the maximum value in the selected range

MIN - Finds the minimum value in the selected range

NOW - Returns current date and time

PMT - Calculates the payment for specific loan terms

SUM - Adds the values in the selected range

SUMIF - Adds together all values that meet specific criteria

TODAY - Returns the current date

VLOOKUP and **HLOOKUP** - Finds a value in a table

Using the Formula Palette with the Function Wizard

Although functions can be typed directly into a cell, the Function Wizard can be used to simplify the process. The Function Wizard leads you through the process of inserting a function.

To use the Function Wizard:

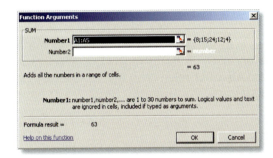

Step 1: Select the cell in which the function is to be inserted.

Step 2: Click the **Insert Function (f$_x$)** button on the Formula bar and the Insert Function dialog box appears.

Step 3: In the **Select a function:** area, select the function to be inserted.

Step 4: If a particular function is not listed in the **Select a function:** area, you may need to select a different category using the **Or select a category:** drop-down list.

Step 5: Click **OK**. The Function Arguments dialog box opens.

Step 6: Enter the arguments for the formula. To select a range of cells as an argument, click the **Collapse Dialog** button in the Number 1 field.

Step 7: After selecting the range, click the **Expand Dialog** button to return to the Formula Palette.

Step 8: Verify that the correct arguments have been recorded.

Step 9: Click **OK** to return to the worksheet and insert the function.

Note - In Step 6 above, depending on the cell chosen for the function, Excel may pre-fill the argument. You can overwrite the pre-filled argument by typing in the correct information or selecting your own group of cells.

Using References

A formula can be moved from one worksheet location to another. When a formula is moved, the cell addresses are automatically changed relative to the location to which they are moved. This is known as Relative referencing. By default, Excel does not treat cells included in the formula as a set location but considers them as a relative location. This type of referencing saves you time, since the same formula need not be created repeatedly. For example, AutoSum formulas are written with relative referencing.

In certain situations, it might be necessary to refer to the same specific cell on the worksheet in every copy of the formula. The Absolute referencing method is used in such cases. Absolute references are denoted by dollar signs before the column and row addresses. For example, $A$2 would be an absolute reference to cell A2.

- An example of a **Relative** reference is =SUM(B2:B6).
- An example of an **Absolute** reference is =SUM($B$2:$B$6).

Using Date Functions

Excel 2003 uses the 1900 date system. It is important to keep the following in mind when working with years that pre-date the year 1900:

- If the year is between 0 (zero) and 1899 (inclusive), Excel adds that value to 1900 to calculate the year. For example, DATE(101,1,2) returns January 2, 2001 (1900+101). In the formula DATE(101,1,2), the single digit 1 equals the month and the single digit 2 equals the day.

- If the year is between 1900 and 9999 (inclusive), Excel uses that value as the year. For example, DATE(2003,1,2) returns January 2, 2003.

To insert the DATE function:

Step 1: Click the cell where you want to add the function.

Step 2: Click the **Insert Function (f$_x$)** button on the Formula bar. The Insert Function dialog box appears.

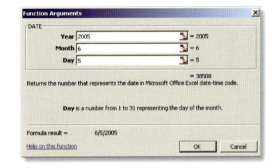

Step 3: In the **Select a function:** area, select **DATE**, and click **OK**. The Function Arguments dialog box opens.

Step 4: Enter the year, month, and day information in the corresponding fields.

Step 5: Click **OK**.

To insert the NOW function:

Step 1: Click the cell where you want to add the function.

Step 2: Click the **Insert Function (f$_x$)** button on the Formula bar. The Insert Function dialog box appears.

Step 3: In the **Select a function:** area, select **Now**, and click **OK**. The Function Arguments dialog box opens.

Step 4: Click **OK**.

Using Financial Functions

The FV function returns the future value of an investment based on periodic, constant payments and a constant interest rate. For example, if you paid 7% interest every year for four years and paid the monthly payment of £285 at the beginning of each period, the formula would read:

=FV(7%/12, 4*12,-285,0,1)

• **Rate** - the interest rate per period; in our example 7% interest per year (12 monthly payments).

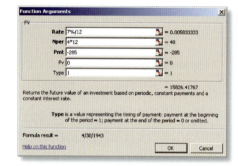

• **Nper** - the total number of payment periods in an annuity; in our example four years is the pay off.

• **Pmt** - the payment made each period, which cannot change over the life of the annuity; £285 monthly payment. (This amount is represented as a negative number.)

• **Pv** - the present value, or lump-sum amount that a series of future payments is worth now. If omitted Pv=0.

• **Type** - a value representing the timing of the payments. Payments at the beginning of the period equal one, payments at the end of the period equal zero, or omitted. If a payment is made at the beginning of the period, it is Type 1.

To insert an FV function:

Step 1: Click the cell where you want to add the function.

Step 2: Click the Insert **Function (f$_x$)** button on the Formula bar. The Insert Function dialog box appears.

Step 3: In the **Select a function:** area, select **FV**, and click **OK**. The Function Arguments dialog box opens.

Step 4: Click **OK** when you have finished entering information into all of the necessary fields.

The PMT function calculates the payment for a loan based on constant payments and a constant interest rate. For example: If you paid five percent interest every year, for five years on a £18,000 loan, with the payments made at the end of each month, the formula would read:

$$=PMT(5\%/12, 5*12, -18000, 0, 0)$$

- **Rate** - 5%/12 (interest rate per year divided by the number of payments per year)

- **Nper** - 5*12 (number of years to pay back the loan multiplied by 12 months)

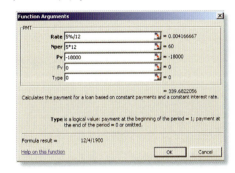

- **Pv** - 18000 (the total payoff amount; remember, this number is entered as a negative number)

- **Fv** - 0 (cash balance attained after the last payment is made)

- **Type** - 0 (Payments made at the end of the period)

To insert a Payment function:

Step 1: Click the cell where you want to add the function.

Step 2: Click the **Insert Function (f$_x$)** button on the Formula bar. The Insert Function dialog box appears.

Step 3: In the **Select a function:** area, select **PMT**, and click **OK**. The Function Arguments dialog box opens.

Step 4: Click **OK** when you have finished entering information.

Using Logical Functions

Suppose that your company determines your 5% or 10% merit raise based on how many sales you made this year. To determine which one of the two raises you will receive, use the IF worksheet function. For example, if you sold more than £130,000 in product this year, you get a £10,000 merit raise. If you sold less than £130,000, you get a £5,000 raise. In this example, the formula would read:

=IF(N3>130000," £10,000"," £5,000")

Logical_Test - N3>130000 (N3 would be the cell containing the amount of product sold this year)
Value_if_true - "£10,000"
Value_if_false - "£5,000"

To insert the IF function:

Step 1: Click the cell where you want to add the function.

Step 2: Click the **Insert Function (f$_x$)** button on the Formula bar. The Insert Function dialog box appears.

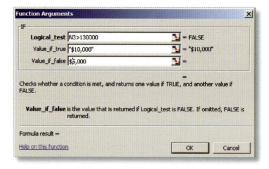

Step 3: In the **Select a function:** area, select **IF**, and click **OK**. The Function Arguments dialog box opens.

Step 4: Click **OK** when you have finished entering information.

Linking Worksheets and Consolidating Data Using 3-D References

Linking information from one worksheet to another can save a great deal of time. Linking allows you to copy information from one worksheet or workbook to another.

To link worksheets and consolidate data:

Step 1: Click the worksheet tab where the linked or consolidated information is to be placed.

Step 2: Select the cells where the information is to be placed.

Step 3: From the **Data** menu, select **Consolidate**.... The Consolidate dialog box appears.

Step 4: Use the drop-down to select the required function.

Step 5: Click in the **Reference:** section.

Step 6: Click on the worksheet tab where the information to be consolidated is located. Excel will make that the active worksheet, and the sheet name will appear in the Reference: section.

Step 7: Select cells you need to link or consolidate. In the Consolidate dialog box, the cell range (reference) will appear after the sheet name in the Reference: section.

Step 8: Click the **Add** button. You will now see the references in the All references: area as well.

Step 9: If additional data needs to be linked or consolidated, repeat Steps 5 through 8.

Step 10: Click the **Create links to source data** box to ensure that changes made to any of the worksheets will automatically update.

Step 11: Click **OK**.

Summary

The key points discussed in this lesson are:

◆ A function is a predefined formula that performs calculations by using specific values, called arguments, in a particular order.

◆ Understanding that although functions can be typed directly into a cell, the Function Wizard can be used to simplify the process by leading us through the step-by-step process of inserting a function.

◆ Deciding when to use Absolute and Relative References.

◆ Using Date Functions enable you to reformat numeric entries.

◆ Using Financial Functions can easily compute complicated financial processes.

◆ Using Logical Functions enables you to create formulas that interpret data and populate a cell with text based on specific true or false statements.

◆ Linking Worksheets and Consolidating Data Using 3-D References allows you to link and copy information from one worksheet to another.

Creating Charts

Charts display statistical information in a graphic, visual form. Charts can be very simple or very complex, depending on the subject matter and the audience. In this lesson, you will learn how to create and format charts. You will also learn how to create an embedded chart and a separate chart sheet.

Objectives

Upon completing this lesson, you will be able to:

- Identify the different types of charts
- Identify parts of a chart
- Create a chart using the Chart wizard
- Format the chart
- Modify the chart

What is a Chart?

It is often easier to grasp data when it is presented graphically rather than as a collection of data listed numerically. A chart is a way to present a table of numbers visually and is based on the data that appears in the worksheet. Displaying data in a well-conceived chart can make it more understandable, allowing you to make your point more quickly.

A chart can use data from any number of worksheets or even from different workbooks. Charts can be separately stored on Chart sheets or can be embedded in the current sheet so that they become a part of it. Both embedded charts and chart sheets are updated as the data on the worksheets is changed.

Types of Charts

The first step in creating a chart is deciding on the data to include in the chart. The second step is to choose the type of chart. There are many different chart types available in Excel 2003. The key ideas to keep in mind when selecting a chart type are:

- The kind of data being used in the chart
- The chart type the audience is accustomed to seeing and interpreting

The different chart types available are:

Column Charts - Column charts are one of the most commonly used types of charts. This type of chart is useful for displaying discrete data. You can have any number of data series, and the columns can be stacked on top of each other.

Bar Charts - A Bar chart is essentially a column chart that has been rotated 90 degrees. Bar charts can consist of any number of data series.

Line Charts - Line charts are used to plot data that is continuous and not discrete.

Pie Chart - A Pie chart is useful when you want to show relative proportions or contributions with respect to a whole entity. Generally, a Pie chart uses no more than five or six data points; otherwise it is difficult for the user to interpret. A Pie chart can use only one data series.

XY (Scatter) Charts - Another common chart type is the XY chart. An XY chart type differs from the other chart types in that both axes display values. This type of chart is often used to show the relationship between two variables.

Area Charts - An Area chart is similar to a Line chart that has been coloured. Stacking the data series lets you clearly see the total plus the contribution by each series.

Doughnut Charts - A Doughnut chart is similar to a pie chart, except that it has a hole in the middle. Unlike a Pie chart, a Doughnut chart can display more than one data series. Data series are displayed as concentric rings. A Doughnut chart with more than one series to chart can be difficult to interpret.

Radar Charts - A Radar chart has a separate axis for each category, and the axis extends out from the centre. The values of the data point are plotted on the appropriate axis. If all data points in a series had an identical value, it would produce a perfect circle.

Surface Charts - Surface charts display two or more data series on a surface. Unlike other charts, Excel uses colour to distinguish values, not to distinguish the data series. The only way to change these colours is to modify the workbook's colour palette by using the colour panel in the Options dialog box.

Bubble Charts - Bubble charts are new in Excel. Additional data series are represented by the size of the bubbles. The chart is displayed in the form of bubbles.

Stock Charts - Stock charts are very useful for displaying stock market information. These charts require three to five data series, depending on the subtype. This chart uses the High-Low-Close subtype that requires three data series.

Cylinder, Cone and Pyramid Charts - These three charts are essentially the same – except for the shapes used. You can use these charts in place of a Bar or Column chart.

Parts of a Chart

The more you understand the various parts of a chart, the easier it will be for you to decide which chart to use, what information to include, and how best to integrate the chart into the worksheet. In Excel, a chart can be either 2-D or 3-D.

The elements of a 2-D chart are:

Y-Axis - The Y–Axis is called the Series or Rank axis. It shows the value of data points that are plotted.

X-Axis - The X-Axis is known as the Category axis. It shows the categories of the data points that are plotted.

Category Names - Category names identify the individual data points and may be dated. The category names are taken from the topmost row or the left-most column, depending on the orientation of the sheet.

Legend - The legend is a table that describes the data series. These labels are attached to the symbol, colour or pattern that is associated with the series and placed on the chart. It is used to differentiate one data series from another.

Data Marker - The Data marker is another tool used to differentiate one data series from another.

Tick Marks - Tick marks are small lines used to divide the two axes and provide scaling.

Gridlines - Gridlines are displayed for both axes to help read the value of individual data points. Gridlines are scaled according to the values on the axis and can be changed.

Data Labels - Data labels are displayed at times to show the value of data point.

Selected Border - A selected border identifies that a particular chart can be sized, moved, or deleted and contains nodes or handles for that purpose.

Additional Elements

In addition to the elements of a 2-D chart, 3-D charts have the following additional elements:

Z-Axis - The Z-Axis is called the "value" axis and shows the value of the data points.

Wall - The wall is the background of the plotted area.

Corners - Corners can be rotated to give different views to the user.

Floor - The floor is the base upon which the series are plotted.

Creating a Chart Using the Chart Wizard

Using the Chart Wizard makes creating a chart a very easy task.

To create a chart using the Chart Wizard:

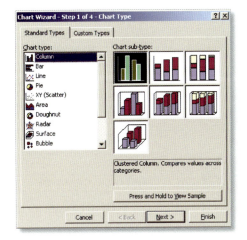

Step 1: Select the cells to display in the chart.

Step 2: On the Standard toolbar, click the **Chart Wizard** button; the Chart Wizard dialog box appears.

Step 3: In the **Chart type:** section, select the chart type.

Step 4: In the **Chart sub-type:** section, select the Chart sub-type.

Step 5: To preview what the chart will look like, click the **Press and Hold to View Sample** button. When the desired chart has been located, click **Next** to continue.

Step 6: The second step of the Chart Wizard gives you many options. Select the required options from both the **Data Range** and **Series** tabs. Click **Next** to continue.

Step 7: The third step of the Chart Wizard also provides you with many options. Enter the chart title and any other required options from the six tabs. Click **Next** to continue.

Step 8: The fourth step asks if the chart is to be placed in as a new sheet or as an object in an existing sheet. If **As new sheet:** is chosen, you have the option of naming the new sheet while still in the Wizard. If **As object in:** is chosen, specify which sheet you want it added to by clicking on the drop-down arrow and selecting the appropriate sheet.

Step 9: Click **Finish** when you have made all selections.

Changing the Chart Type

After creating a chart, you might feel that a different chart type would display data better.

To change the Chart Type:

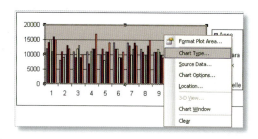

Step 1: Right-click the chart.

Step 2: Select **Chart Type**... from the menu that appears. The Chart Type dialog box opens.

Step 3: Select a chart type. Click **OK**.

Note - To undo the chart type change, click the Undo button on the Standard toolbar.

Formatting the Chart

You can format the colour and text style of the chart to draw attention to key parts of the chart.

To format the Data Series in the chart:

Step 1: Double-click directly on a data plot in the chart. The Format Data Series dialog box opens.

Step 2: In the Format Data Series dialog box, click the **Patterns** tab.

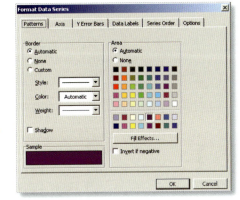

Step 3: In the **Border** section, change the border colour, style, and thickness by clicking the drop-down menu to the right of the **Style:, Colour:,** or **Weight:** options.

Step 4: In the **Area** section, change the colour of the data representation.

Step 5: Click **OK**. Follow the same procedure to format the remainder of the chart.

To format the text in the chart:

Step 1: Double-click directly on the text to be changed.

Step 2: In the Format Axis dialog box, click the **Font** tab.

Step 3: From the various menus, select the font, font style, colour, size, and other attributes to use.

Step 4: Click **OK**.

Changing the Chart Data

The data in a chart is updated automatically when the values in a source range changes, but if you add any extra cells, rows, or columns into the worksheet, those changes will not be reflected in the chart. There are two ways you can change source range:

- Change the data range in the Source Range dialog box.
- Change the source range by re-selecting the cells in the worksheet, including the new cells, and using the Chart wizard to build a new chart. If you have not spent a great deal of time formatting the chart with new colours and text style, this is often the easiest method to use.

To change the chart data using the Source Range dialog box:

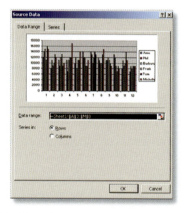

Step 1: Right-click the chart.

Step 2: Select **Source Data** from the pop-up menu.

Step 3: If the chart is on its own worksheet, the workbook will revert to the worksheet from which the chart was initially created. To figure out how to change the data range, look for the names of the following two cells:

- The cell in the upper left corner of the cells you want to include in the chart.
- The cell in the bottom right corner of the cells you want to include in the chart.

Step 4: In the **Data range:** section, verify the formula that indicates the cells currently contained in the chart.

Step 5: Click **OK.**

Summary

The key points discussed in this lesson are:

◆ Learning that a chart is a way to present a table of numbers visually and is based on the data that appears in the worksheet.

◆ Learning the various types of charts and what chart might best suit the data.

◆ Learning the parts of a chart so that it will be easier for you to decide which chart to use, what information to include, and how best to integrate the chart into the worksheet.

◆ Creating a chart using the Chart Wizard.

◆ Changing the type of chart you are using if you feel that a different chart type would display the data better.

◆ Formatting the colour and text style of the chart to reflect your own personality or to draw attention to key parts of the chart.

◆ Updating the information in the chart if you need to add any extra cells, rows, or columns into the worksheet.

Adding Clip Art

Using Clip Art can greatly enhance a worksheet. With the careful selection of appropriate graphics you can enhance key points, add humour and highlight special sections of the worksheet. Clip Art can also add a personal touch to the worksheet separating your work from the work of others by making it distinctly your style.

Objectives

Upon completing this lesson, you will be able to:

- ✔ Insert Clip Art
- ✔ Edit Clip Art
- ✔ Move Clip Art
- ✔ Delete Clip Art

Inserting Clip Art

A Clip Art image is a drawing that can be used to suggest a topic, or to enhance a list or other text display. Microsoft's Clip Art Gallery provides a generous library of clip art, sounds, and motion clips from which to choose. The Clip Art Gallery contains images of animals, people, household objects, cartoons, etc. It also gives you quick link buttons to import clips, acquire clips online, or search for help.

To insert Clip Art into the worksheet:

Step 1: From the **Insert** menu, select **Picture**. From the pop-up list, select Clip Art. The **Clip Art** task pane appears.

Step 2: Type an entry in the **Search for** text box and click the **Go** button. Images will appear in the lower part of the pane.

Step 3: Double-click your image of choice or select the side arrow when you roll over the image and click **Insert**.

The Clip Art task pane remains open so that you can add more Clip Art to the worksheet. Add as many pieces of Clip Art as you want and then close the task pane by clicking the X in the upper right corner of the task pane.

Resizing Clip Art

Clip Art can be resized to fit properly into the worksheet.

To resize Clip Art:

Step 1: Click the Clip Art object.

Step 2: Drag a corner selection handle towards the centre of the object to reduce the size of the object.

Step 3: Drag a corner selection handle away from the centre of the object to enlarge the size of the object.

Note - An easy way to make a copy of the Clip Art is to press and hold the Ctrl key while dragging the object. If you continue to hold the Ctrl key, each time you release the mouse a new copy of the Clip Art will appear.

Moving and Deleting Clip Art

Once you learn how to move and delete Clip Art, you will be able to move or delete any kind of graphic, chart or picture from the worksheets.

To move Clip Art or any inserted object:

Step 1: Click and hold the object to be moved.

Step 2: Use the mouse to move it to the location of your choice and then release the mouse button.

OR

Step 1: Single-click the object to be moved.

Step 2: Use the arrow keys on the keyboard to move it around the worksheet.

To delete Clip Art or any inserted object:

Step 1: Single-click the object to be deleted.

Step 2: Press the **Delete** key on the keyboard.

Summary

The key points discussed in this lesson are:

- ◆ Inserting Clip Art to help make a point, add humour, and make the worksheet more interesting.

- ◆ Resizing Clip Art so that it fits properly into the worksheet.

- ◆ Moving Clip Art to other locations within your workbook and deleting Clip Art that you feel does not add value to the workbook.

Inserting and Formatting Objects

Another way of making a worksheet interesting is to add drawing objects and text boxes. Much like using Clip Art, using objects in the worksheet can add humour, enhance a key point, and make the worksheet fun and interesting. This lesson covers how to create your own shapes and add existing shapes to the worksheet.

Objectives

Upon completing this lesson, you will be able to:

- ✔ Use the Drawing toolbar
- ✔ Draw shapes and AutoShapes
- ✔ Format shapes
- ✔ Add text to AutoShapes
- ✔ Create and edit text boxes
- ✔ Resize and move objects

The Drawing Toolbar

The Drawing toolbar gives you a wide variety of graphics, formats, and design tools to enhance the worksheet. You can access the Drawing toolbar by clicking the Drawing button on the Standard toolbar.

Some of the more commonly used features of the Drawing Toolbar are designed to:

• Change an object's fill, line, and shadow colour	• Add AutoShapes
• Draw lines and arrows in different styles	• Draw circles and squares
• Group and ungroup objects	• Add text boxes
• Flip objects	

Drawing Shapes

To draw straight lines:

Step 1: On the Drawing toolbar, click or double-click the **Line** tool. Clicking once on the tool allows you draw a single line only. Double-clicking allows you to draw multiple lines.

Step 2: Click and drag on the worksheet to draw the line. Release the mouse button.

To draw rectangles and squares:

Step 1: On the Drawing toolbar, click/double-click on the **Rectangle** tool to select it.

Step 2: Click and drag on the worksheet to draw the rectangle or square.

Step 3: If you want to draw a perfect square, first hold down the **Shift** key and while holding it, click and drag on the worksheet. Release the mouse button.

To draw ovals and circles:

Step 1: On the Drawing toolbar, click/double-click the **Oval** tool to select it.

Step 2: Click and drag on the worksheet to draw the oval. Release the mouse button.

Step 3: To draw a perfect circle, first hold down the **Shift** key and while holding it, click and drag onto the slide.

Drawing AutoShapes

Excel comes with a set of ready-made shapes called AutoShapes that can be used in the worksheets. The shapes can be resized, rotated, flipped, coloured, and combined with other shapes to make more complex shapes.

The AutoShapes menu on the Drawing toolbar contains several categories of shapes, including **Lines, Connectors, Basic Shapes, Block Arrows, Flowcharts, Stars and Banners, Callouts,** and **Action Buttons**. There also is an option called More AutoShapes. When you use this option, the Clip Art task pane opens with more AutoShapes displayed.

To draw a bevel:

Step 1: On the Drawing toolbar, click the **AutoShapes** button and then select **Basic Shapes**. Select the **Bevel** tool.

Step 2: Click and drag over the worksheet to draw a bevel.

Step 3: If you want to draw a perfectly square bevel, first hold down the **Shift** key, and while holding it, click and drag onto the worksheet.

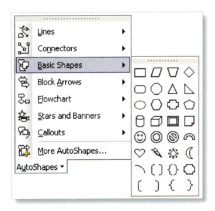

To draw a star:

Step 1: On the Drawing toolbar, click the **AutoShapes** button and then select **Stars and Banners**. Select one of the **Star** options.

Step 2: Click and drag over the worksheet to draw a star.

Step 3: If you want to draw a perfect star, first hold down the **Shift** key, and while holding it, click and drag onto the worksheet.

Formatting Shapes

To change the fill colour of a shape or an AutoShape:

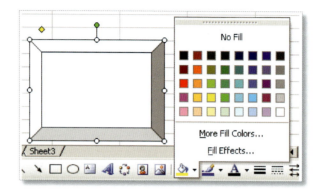

Step 1: Click the shape.

Step 2: On the Drawing toolbar, click the down arrow located on the right side of the **Fill Color** button.

Step 3: From the pop-up colour list, select the colour you want to use.

To change the line colour of a shape or an AutoShape:

Step 1: Click the shape.

Step 2: On the **Drawing** toolbar, click the down arrow located on the right side of the **Line Colour** button.

Step 3: From the pop-up colour list, select the colour you wish to use.

Adding Text to AutoShapes

To include text in the AutoShape:

Step 1: Right-click the AutoShape and select **Add Text**.

Step 2: Type the text inside the shape.

Step 3: Click outside the AutoShape to end typing.

Resizing Objects

Excel enables you to resize objects quickly and easily to make them fit properly in a worksheet.

To resize an object:

Step 1: Select the object.

Step 2: Drag a selection handle towards the centre of the object to reduce the size of the object.

Step 3: Drag a selection handle away from the centre of the object to increase its size.

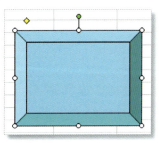

Step 4: If you want to resize the object and maintain proportions, hold down the Shift key, and click and drag the object to the desired size.

Creating Text Boxes

Text boxes can be used as a label or explanation to accompany any graphics included in the worksheet.

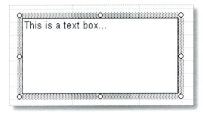

To create a textbox:

Step 1: On the Drawing toolbar, click the **Text Box** tool to select it. Position the mouse pointer where you want the text to begin.

Step 2: Click and drag to create a text object that wraps the words automatically.

Step 3: Enter the desired text. Once the typing is completed, click outside the text box.

Editing Text

Editing the text to include different colours and font styles can make the worksheet more appealing. Excel text formatting includes font name, size, style, justification, colour, and many other options. Text formats can be changed by selecting/highlighting the text and applying the desired formatting.

To change the style of the text:

Step 1: Using the mouse, select/highlight the desired text.

Step 2: Click the desired text-editing button on the Formatting toolbar or press its corresponding keyboard shortcut: **Ctrl + B** to make the text bold; **Ctrl + I** to change the style to italic; or **Ctrl + U** to underline.

To change the colour of the text:

Step 1: Using the mouse, select/highlight the desired text.

Step 2: On the Drawing toolbar, click the down arrow located on the right side of the **Font Colour** button.

Step 3: From the pop-up colour list, select the colour you wish to use.

Moving Objects and Text Boxes

To move an object or a text box, click and hold the object, and then drag it to its new location.

To move objects in small increments:

Step 1: Click directly on the object.

Step 2: Press the arrow keys on the keyboard (left, right, up or down).

To move text boxes in small increments:

Step 1: Click directly on the outline of the textbox.

Step 2: Press the arrow keys on the keyboard (left, right, up or down).

To move objects and text boxes one pixel at a time:

Step 1: Click directly on the object or on the outline of the text box.

Step 2: Hold the **Ctrl** key while pressing the arrow keys on the keyboard (left, right, up or down).

Summary

The key points discussed in this lesson are:

◆ The Drawing toolbar gives you a wide variety of graphics, formats, and design tools to enhance the worksheet.

◆ Drawing shapes and AutoShapes to enhance the content of the worksheet.

◆ Formatting shapes and AutoShapes so that their appearance properly reflects the key points in the worksheet.

◆ Adding text to AutoShapes to make the shapes more meaningful.

◆ Resizing objects so that they fit properly into the worksheet.

◆ Creating text boxes that add important information to the worksheet.

◆ Editing text to include different colours and font styles that make the worksheet more appealing.

◆ Moving objects and text boxes to the appropriate location in the worksheet.

Saving a Workbook

In this lesson, you will learn how to save a workbook in a variety of formats.

Objectives

Upon completing this lesson, you will be able to:

- ✔ Save a workbook
- ✔ Save the workbook as a Web page
- ✔ Send the workbook via e-mail

Saving a Workbook

You have several options when saving a workbook. You learned earlier how to save a workbook as a template. In this lesson you will learn how to save it as a regular Excel workbook.

To save the workbook for the first time:

Step 1: From the **File** menu, select **Save As**. The Save As dialog box appears.

Step 2: In the Save As dialog box, using the **Save in**: drop-down menu, select the location to save the workbook.

Step 3: In the **File name**: field, type in the name of the workbook.

Step 4: Click **Save**.

 Note - It is highly recommended that you save the workbook every 5-10 minutes to ensure that in the event of something unexpected you do not lose valuable work.

To re-save the worksheet:

- On the Standard toolbar, click the **Save** button.

OR

- From the **File** menu, select **Save**.

Saving a Workbook as a Web page

To save the worksheet as a webpage:

Step 1: From the **File** menu, select **Save as Web Page**. The Save As dialog box will appear.

Step 2: In the Save As dialog box, using the **Save in**: drop-down menu, select the location to save the workbook.

Step 3: In the File Name field, type in the name of the workbook.

Step 4: In the **Save** section, click the radio button that corresponds with your choice to either save the entire workbook as a web page, or only the selected sheet (the worksheet you are currently viewing).

Step 5: Click **Save**.

 Note - You also have the option to make the saved workbook or worksheet interactive. Making the workbook or worksheet interactive means that it can be edited while being viewed as a webpage.

Sending a Workbook via E-mail

A very convenient feature of Excel is the ability to send the workbook via e-mail without having to open the default e-mail application.

To send the workbook via e-mail:

Step 1: From the **File** menu, select **Send To**.

Step 2: From the **Send To** pop-up list, select **Mail Recipient**.

Step 3: The E-mail dialogue box will appear. Select whether you want to: send the current sheet as the message body, or send the entire workbook as an attachment.

Step 4: After you have made your selection, click **OK**. After you click OK, Excel opens your e-mail application with the workbook inserted into a new mail message.

Step 5: Enter the e-mail address you would like to send the workbook to, add a subject (a default subject with the name of the workbook will be auto filled, but you may change it to whatever you like) and any body text you would like to enter.

Step 6: When you are finished, click **Send**.

Summary

The key points discussed in this lesson are:

◆ Saving a workbook using both the Menu bar and the Standard toolbar.

◆ Saving a workbook as a webpage so that it can be published on the Internet.

◆ Sending a workbook via e-mail as an attachment or as the message body.

Setting up a Workbook

In this lesson, you will learn how to properly set up the page so that the worksheet prints out in the most effective manner.

Objectives

Upon completing this lesson, you will be able to:

✔ Preview the workbook before printing

✔ Insert, remove and view page breaks

✔ Change the orientation and scale of the workbook

✔ Set margins, headers and footers

Previewing a Workbook

Previewing a workbook allows you to see how it will look when it is printed. Based on the preview, you may need to edit the worksheet or adjust the page margins so that it prints the way you want it to look.

To preview the workbook:

Step 1: From the **File** menu, select **Print Preview**.

Step 2: If the worksheet is more than one page, use the scroll bar on the right side of the screen to view additional pages.

Step 3: Click the **Close** button to return to the worksheet.

To preview the workbook as a Web page:

Step 1: From the **File** menu, select **Web Page Preview**.

Step 2: A new window opens that allows you to see what the workbook looks like as a Web page.

Inserting, Removing, and Viewing Page Breaks

Page breaks set how many rows and columns in the worksheet will fit onto each printed page.

To insert Page breaks:

Step 1: From the **Insert** menu, select **Page Break**.

Step 2: Dashed lines will appear on the worksheets to indicate page breaks.

To remove Page breaks:

Step 1: Click a cell just to the right of the vertical page break or click a cell just below the horizontal page break.

Step 2: From the Insert menu, select **Remove Page Break**.

To remove all manual Page breaks:

Step 1: From the **View** menu, select **Page Break Preview**.

Step 2: Right-click on any cell in the worksheet.

Step 3: From the **Shortcut** menu, select **Reset All Page Breaks**.

Changing Page Orientation and Scaling

Excel allows you to print the worksheet in either Portrait orientation (vertical) or Landscape orientation (horizontal).

To change page orientation:

Step 1: From the **File** menu, select **Page Setup....**

Step 2: Make sure the **Page** tab is selected.

Step 3: In the Orientation section, click to the radio button for either **Portrait** or **Landscape.**

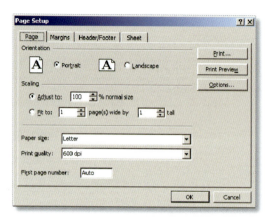

Step 4: To preview what the worksheet will look like in either orientation, click the **Print Preview** button. This may help you decide which orientation to use. To get back to the Page Setup, click the **Setup** button in the **Print Preview** window.

Step 5: Click **OK** from Page Setup or **Close** from Print Preview.

To adjust the scaling of the worksheet:

Step 1: From the **File** menu, select **Page Setup**.

Step 2: Make sure the **Page** tab is selected.

Step 3: In the Scaling section you have the following options:

- Click the radio button next to **Adjust to**: and then use the up/down arrows to select a size either larger or smaller than the current 100% scaling.
- Click the **Print Preview** button to view how the scaling change affects the way the worksheet prints.

OR

- Click the radio button next to **Fit to:** and select how many pages wide and how many pages tall you wish to fit onto one printed sheet.
- Click the **Print Preview** button to see how the Fit to: change affects the way the worksheet prints.

Setting Page Margins

The worksheet may be too large to print on one sheet of paper by only a column or row. In that case, you may want to adjust the margins so that the entire worksheet fits on the printed page. You may also choose to have the worksheet centered on the printed page either horizontally or vertically, or both.

To set margins:

Step 1: From the **File** menu, select **Page Setup**. The Page Setup dialog box will appear.

Step 2: Click on the **Margins** tab.

Step 3: Choose which margins you want to change: Top, bottom, right or left. Using the up/down arrows, adjust the margins either smaller or larger.

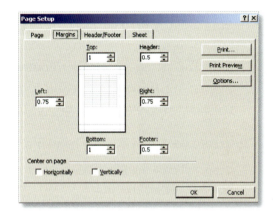

Step 4: Click the **Print Preview** button to see how the new margins affect the way the worksheet will print. To get back to the Page Setup, click the **Setup** button in the **Print Preview** window.

Step 5: Click **OK** from Page Setup or **Close** from Print Preview.

To centre the worksheet:

Step 1: From the **File** menu, select **Page Setup**. The Page Setup dialog box will appear.

Step 2: Click on the **Margins** tab.

Step 3: At the bottom of the **Margins** tab are the options for centring the page.

Step 4: Click the horizontal and/or vertical radio buttons to centre the page.

Step 5: Click the **Print Preview** button to see how centring affects the way the worksheet prints.

Step 6: Click the **Setup** button in the Print Preview window to reopen the Page Setup dialog box.

Step 7: Click **OK**.

Headers and Footers

Adding a header and/or footer to a workbook can help keep the printed worksheets organised. You can choose to add page numbers, your name, or company information to each page. You could either choose one of the already existing headers or footers or you may create your own.

To choose a default header and/or footer:

Step 1: From the **File** menu, select **Page Setup**. The Page Setup dialog box will appear.

Step 2: Click on the **Header/Footer** tab.

Step 3: The **Header:** and **Footer:** sections have drop-down menus with pre-selected options. Click on the header and/or footer you want to use.

To create your own custom header and/or footer:

Step 1: From the **File** menu, select **Page Setup**. The Page Setup dialog box will appear.

Step 2: Click on the **Header/Footer** tab.

Step 3: Click on the **Custom Header** or **Custom Footer** button. A Header or Footer dialog box will appear.

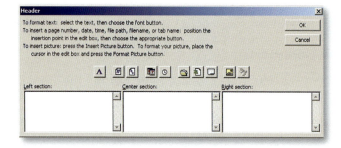

Step 4: The dialog box provides three options as to where the header/footer information will appear on the page: **Left section:**, **Centre section:** and **Right section:**. Click into the section where you want to place the information.

Step 5: You may choose the following default items to appear in the header or footer by clicking on the corresponding button:

• Text	• Page Number
• Total number of pages in worksheet	• Date
• Time	• File path or file name
• Tab name	• Picture

Step 6: To enter custom text, click on the **Text** button (looks like the letter "A"). The Font dialogue box will appear.

Step 7: Select the formatting you want for the text.

Step 8: Click **OK** to close the Font dialogue box.

Step 9: Then enter the text into the section in which you want the text to appear.

Step 10: Click **OK**.

Step 11: Click the **Print Preview** button to see how the header and/or footer will look on the printed worksheet. To return to the Page Setup, click the **Setup** button in the **Print Preview** window.

Step 12: Click **OK** from Page Setup or **Close** from Print Preview.

Summary

The key points discussed in this lesson are:

◆ Previewing a workbook allows you to see how it will look when it is printed so that you may make any necessary adjustments.

◆ Add page breaks so that you can see how many rows and columns in the worksheet will fit onto each printed page.

◆ Change page orientation and scaling so that your worksheet prints according to your specifications.

◆ Set page margins so that the entire worksheet fits on the printed page.

◆ Insert headers and footers that could contain page numbers, your name, or company information to each page in the workbook.

Printing the Workbook

In this lesson, you will learn how to effectively print workbooks.

Objectives

Upon completing this lesson, you will be able to:

- ✔ Set print titles and options
- ✔ Print only a selected portion of a worksheet
- ✔ Print the worksheet

Setting Print Titles and Options

If you are working with a large worksheet that will print on more than one page, you may wish to repeat the title cell at the top of each printed page.

To Print row and column labels on every page:

Step 1: Click the worksheet you want to set up.

Step 2: From the **File** menu, select **Page Setup**, and then click on the **Sheet** tab.

Step 3: In the **Print titles** section, in the **Rows to repeat at top:** section, click on the **Collapse Dialog** button.

Step 4: The active worksheet becomes visible. Select the cells to have repeated at the top of each printed page. This will often be the Title cell of the worksheet. In the small dialog box that is visible: **Page Setup - Rows to repeat at top:**, you will see the name and/or range of cells selected to appear at the top of each printed page.

Step 5: Click the **Expand Dialog** button again to close the dialog box and return to Page Setup. The names/range of the cells selected are now in the **Rows to repeat at top:** field.

Step 6: Follow the same procedure to select **Columns to repeat at left:**.

Step 7: Click the **Print Preview** button to see how the printed page will look with the repeating rows and/or columns. To get back to the Page Setup, click the **Setup** button in the **Print Preview** window.

Step 8: Click **OK** from Page Setup or **Close** from Print Preview.

Printing Only a Section of the Worksheet

You may have an elaborate worksheet that contains a great deal of information, but you only want to print out a small section of it to disperse to your co-workers. Excel allows you to print out only those rows and columns that you wish to share.

To print only a section of the worksheet:

Step 1: Click the worksheet you want to set up.

Step 2: From the **File** menu, select **Page Setup**, and then click on the **Sheet** tab.

Step 3: In the **Print area:** section, click on the **Collapse Dialog** button.

Step 4: The active worksheet will become visible. Select the cells you want to print.

Step 5: Click the **Expand Dialog** button again to close the dialog box and return to Page Setup.

Step 6: The name/range of the cells you selected are now filled into the **Print area:** field.

Step 7: Click the **Print Preview** button to see how the printed page will look.

Step 8: Click **Close** to return to the worksheet or click **Setup** to return to the **Page Setup** dialog box.

Printing the Workbook

Now that you have selected all of your page setup options, it is time to print the workbook.

To print a worksheet or the entire workbook:

Step 1: From the **File** menu, select **Print….**

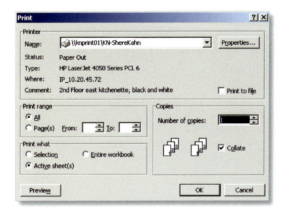

Step 2: In the **Print what** section, select whether you wish to print the **Selection** of cells you chose in Page setup, the **Entire workbook,** or the **Active sheet(s)**.

Step 3: In the **Print range** section, choose whether or not you want to print all or only a certain number of pages. If you choose to only print a select group of pages, use the up/down arrows to select the pages you wish to print.

Step 4: In the **Copies** section, use the up/down arrows to select how many copies of the worksheet you want to print.

Step 5: Click **OK.**

Summary

The key points discussed in this lesson are:

- Setting print titles and options in order to repeat the title cell at the top of each printed page.

- Printing out a section of the worksheet that shows only the rows and columns that you wish to share.

- Printing the entire workbook, only the active sheet, or only a specific selection of cells.

Microsoft Excel 2003 Expert Skills

Module 3: Customising Excel

This module contains information that enables you to customise the way you use Excel to your own, specific requirements. You will learn how to share information with other applications and other users.

Objectives

Upon completing this module, you will be able to:

- ✔ Customise toolbars
- ✔ Use templates
- ✔ Work with named ranges
- ✔ Import and export data
- ✔ Format numbers
- ✔ Collaborate with workgroups

Outline

This module contains these lessons:

- ➤ Working with Toolbars
- ➤ Using Templates
- ➤ Working with Named Ranges
- ➤ Importing and Exporting Data
- ➤ Formatting Numbers
- ➤ Collaborating with Workgroups

Working with Toolbars

Using toolbars is a quick and easy way to perform common tasks in Excel. The Excel application has many pre-defined toolbars. In addition, Excel provides the option of customising existing toolbars or assigning macros to a button that can perform a specific task that you delineate.

Objectives

Upon completing this lesson, you will be able to:

- ✔ Hide and display toolbars
- ✔ Customise a toolbar
- ✔ Move a toolbar

Hiding and Displaying Toolbars

Excel comes equipped with standard toolbars that contain commonly used functions and features. As you use Excel, toolbars are often displayed in relation to the operation you are performing. These toolbars appear as floating palettes. You have the option of hiding, moving, or customising the floating palettes.

To display a toolbar:

Step 1: Select **View > Toolbars.**

Step 2: From the drop-down list, select the desired toolbar.

Step 3: The toolbar is displayed as a floating palette.

To hide a toolbar:

Select **View > Toolbars.**
From the drop-down list, select the desired toolbar to hide.

The toolbar is removed from the Excel application window.

 Note - Toolbars with a check mark next to them are currently visible in the Excel application window.

Customising a Toolbar

Common toolbars, such as the Standard toolbar or the Formatting toolbar, come with a wide variety of features. Some of these features are displayed on the toolbar by default; other features can be added. Customising a toolbar to reflect the functions that you commonly use is an easy way of making the shortcut features in Excel work effectively for you.

To add or remove buttons:

Step 1: On the desired toolbar, click the **Toolbar Options** button.

Step 2: Select **Add or Remove Buttons**, and then select the name of the toolbar (for example, for the Formatting toolbar, you will select **Formatting)**.

Step 3: The drop-down list displays all of the features available on the toolbar. The buttons that are currently visible on the toolbar are labelled with a check mark. Click the name of the feature to add to the toolbar.

Step 4: A check mark appears next to your selection.

Step 5: When you have finished making your selections, click anywhere on your worksheet to close the **Add or Remove Buttons** drop-down list.

To reset a toolbar to its default features:

Step 1: On the desired toolbar, click the **Toolbar Options** button.

Step 2: Select **Add or Remove Buttons** and then the name of the toolbar.

Step 3: Select **Reset Toolbar.**

To create a custom toolbar:

Step 1: On the desired toolbar, click the **Toolbar Options** button.

Step 2: Select **Add or Remove Buttons.**

Step 3: Select **Customise**.

Step 4: Click the **Toolbars** tab.

Step 5: The Toolbars: section lists all pre-defined toolbars.

Step 6: Click **New.**

Step 7: The New Toolbar dialog box displays. Type in a name for the new, custom toolbar and then click **OK.**

Step 8: A small, empty toolbar appears in the application window.

Step 9: In the **Customise** dialog box, click the **Commands** tab.

Step 10: The **Categories:** section lists toolbar features broken down by task.

Step 11: Click a Category title to view the available toolbar elements in the **Commands:** section.

Step 12: To select the commands that you would like to add to your custom toolbar, click and drag the command directly onto your floating toolbar. The command is displayed automatically.

Step 13: To finish your custom toolbar, from the **Customise** dialog box, click the **Options** tab.

Step 14: In the **Other** section, place a check mark next to any options you wish to activate.

Step 15: Click **Close** when you have made all of your selections.

Moving a Toolbar

In most cases, when you add a toolbar to the application window, it initially appears as a floating palette. You may want to anchor that palette to another toolbar so that it does not cover any part of your worksheet. To anchor a floating palette to an anchored toolbar:

Step 1: Click and hold the title bar of the toolbar.

Step 2: Drag the toolbar to the right edge of an anchored toolbar, such as the Standard toolbar.

Step 3: Release the mouse button.

The toolbar should now reside next to the anchored toolbar.

To move a toolbar:

Step 1: Click and hold the vertical grey bar on the left side of the toolbar to move.

Step 2: Drag the toolbar to the desired location.

Step 3: Release the mouse button.

Summary

The key points discussed in this lesson are:

◆ You can hide and display toolbars so that only the toolbars you use often are visible.

◆ You can customise a toolbar to include commonly used features.

◆ You can easily move a toolbar to a more convenient place in the Excel application window.

Using Templates

Working with Excel templates can be a timesaving way of creating worksheets that will be used numerous times, by a variety of people. By creating a custom template, you can establish guidelines and ensure accuracy for topics such as: expense reports, paid time off, invoices and purchase orders.

Objectives

Upon completing this lesson, you will be able to:

✔ Open and apply a template

✔ Edit and save a template

✔ Create a template

Opening and Applying a Template

Excel provides several sample templates. Each template contains a sample of the finished template and a customisable template on which you can practice.

To open the Sales Invoice template:

Step 1: Select **File > New.**

Step 2: From the **New Workbook** task pane, select **On my computer....**

Step 3: From the **Spreadsheet Solutions** tab, select **Sales Invoice.**

 Note - You may receive a Macros dialog box that asks you to Enable or Disable Macros. You must click Enable Macros to open this template. Check with your employer to verify that it is safe to enable macros before doing so.

Step 4: Click **Enable Macros.**

Step 5: The Invoice worksheet opens at the default Invoice tab. The Invoice tab displays the finished worksheet product. The **Customise Your Invoice** tab is used to input your personalised information.

Step 6: The Invoice toolbar initially appears as a floating toolbar. You may move it by dragging it to a more convenient location.

Step 7: Click the Customise Your Invoice tab.

Step 8: Cells with a red triangle include comments that contain helpful information. Hover your cursor above the red triangle to read the comment.

Step 9: In the Type Company Information Here… section, type your company information into the appropriate cell.

Step 10: In the Specify Default Invoice Information Here…section, enter required information.

Step 11: In the Formatted Information: section, notice that the company name and address information you entered in the Type Company Information Here… section is displayed automatically.

Step 12: To format the font, click the **Change Plate Font** button. The Format Cells dialog box opens.

Step 13: Select the formatting to apply.

Step 14: Click **OK.**

Step 15: To add a logo, click the **Select Logo** button. **The Insert Picture** dialog box opens.

Step 16: From the **Look in** drop-down list, select the folder where the logo resides.

Step 17: Click the logo and then click **OK.**

Step 18: To view the custom template, click the **Invoice** tab.

Step 19: To make any changes to the new template, click the **Customise** button to return to **Customise Your Invoice** tab.

 Note - An additional feature in this template is the ability to lock the worksheet. Place your cursor on the red triangle to the right of the Lock/ Save Sheet button for more details.

Editing and Saving a Template

Knowing how to edit a template provides the ability to update and change information contained within the worksheet on an on-going basis.

 Note - Continue using the Invoice template to practice editing a template.

To edit a template:

Step 1: Click the tab of the worksheet to make changes.

Step 2: Click the cell(s) to make changes. Changes can include:

- Formatting text styles
- Adding/changing borders
- Adding colour to cells
- Adding formulas
- Adding graphics or objects

Step 3: Make desired changes.

To save a template:

Step 4: Select **File > Save As.**

Step 5: The **Template File – Save to Database** dialog box appears.

Step 6: Select **Create a New Record**.

Step 7: Click **OK.**

Step 8: The **Save As** dialog box appears.

Step 9: Select the folder to save the template.

Step 10: Name the template.

Step 11: In the **Save as Type** drop-down box, select **Template (*.xlt).**

Step 12: Click **Save.**

Creating a Template

Customising an existing template can help streamline work requirements, such as filling in an expense report. But, you may need to create a worksheet that is customised to a specific procedure or task performed within your company. Creating a template is simply a matter of building a worksheet or workbook that contains formatting, formulas, and procedural requirements and then saving it as a template.

Once you finish creating the workbook, a convenient place to save the template is in Excel's template folder. By saving the template in Excel's template folder, you can easily access it when you open Excel.

To save a template in the template folder:

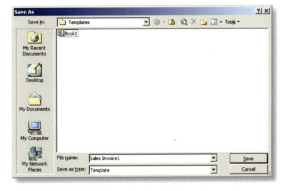

Step 1: Select **File > Save As.**

Step 2: The Look in drop-down menu may default to Microsoft's Templates folder. If not, navigate to: C:\Program Files\Microsoft Office\Templates\1003.

Step 3: Name the template.

Step 4: In the Save as type: drop-down box, select **Template (*.xlt).**

Step 5: Click **Save.**

 Note - Keep in mind that saving a template to this location places it on the hard drive of your individual computer. If you want your template available to all employees, check with your employer to identify a folder that all employees have access to, then save your template in that location.

Summary
The key points discussed in this lesson are:

◆ Excel allows you to open and apply a template to your wordbook.

◆ You can easily edit and save the template.

◆ You can create a template that contains formatting, formulas and procedural requirements specific to your needs.

Working with Named Ranges

An easy way of referencing a group of cells is to give it a name. Giving ranges easy-to-remember names makes creating formulas a simpler process because you do not have to manually select a range of cells each time you want to manipulate it.

Objectives

Upon completing this lesson, you will be able to:

✔ Add a named range

✔ Use a named range in a formula

✔ Use the **HLOOKUP** and **VLOOKUP** functions

Adding a Named Range

Creating a named range of cells makes referencing specific topics within your worksheet an easy task. Keep these formatting requirements in mind when creating a name for the cell range:

- A range name must begin with a letter, unless you use an underscore immediately followed by a number or letter.
- Range names cannot contain spaces. Use an underscore in place of a space.
- Range names cannot look like cell names. For example, you cannot name a range "B7".
- Except for the letters R and C, you can use only one letter to name ranges.

To name a range of cells using adjacent cell labels:

Step 1: Select the cells to include in the range.

Step 2: Select **Insert > Name > Create….** The Create Names dialog box appears.

Step 3: Depending on where the title/heading of the selected cells is located, click the appropriate **Create names in** column or row check box.

Step 4: Excel will automatically name the range based on your selection of cells.

To name a range of cells using Define Name:

Step 1: Select the cells to include in the range.

Step 2: Select **Insert > Name > Define….** The **Define Name** dialog box appears.

Step 3: In the **Names in workbook:** field, type the name of the range, and then click **OK.**

To name a range of cells using the Name box:

Step 1: Select the cells to include in the range.

Step 2: Click the **Name** box.

Step 3: Type the name of the range and press **Enter.**

Using a Named Range in a Formula

Creating a named range of cells is very useful when creating formulas.

To use a named range in a formula:

Step 1: Click the cell where the formula is to reside.

Step 2: Select **Insert > Name > Paste...**. The Paste Name dialog box appears.

Step 3: From the list of range names, click on the desired name, and then click **OK.**

Step 4: Add the operator to the formula, and then select **Insert > Name > Paste...** and click the range to add to the formula. Click **OK**.

Step 5: Repeat these steps until all ranges are added, and then click **Enter** to tabulate the formula.

Using Lookup Functions

HLOOKUP and **VLOOKUP** are used to locate a specific value from within a table or array. **HLOOKUP** searches a spreadsheet horizontally, and **VLOOKUP** searches vertically.

The syntax for **HLOOKUP** is:
HLOOKUP(lookup_val, table_arr, row_idx_num, range_lookup)

The syntax for **VLOOKUP** is:
VLOOKUP(lookup_val, table_arr, col_idx_num, range_lookup)

The lookup_val is the value to locate, and can be a value, text string, or reference. The row_idx_num and col_idx_num designate the row or column of the table from which the value will be returned.

 Note - The Lookup Wizard is an Excel add-in. To add the Lookup Wizard, select **Tools > Add-ins**. Click the check box next to **Lookup Wizard**, and then click **OK.**

To create a lookup function:

Step 1: Select **Tools > Lookup**. The Lookup Wizard dialog box appears.

Step 2: In the **Where is the range to search, including the row and column labels?** section, click the collapse dialog button, and select the range in your worksheet. Click the expand dialog button and then click **Next**.

Step 3: In the next step, select which column and row contains the value to find by clicking the corresponding down arrows and making a selection from the available options. Click **Next**.

Step 4: In step three, select whether you want to copy the formula to a single cell or copy the formula and lookup parameters. Click **Next**. (If you select Copy the formula and lookup parameters, the wizard becomes a six-step process instead of four steps.)

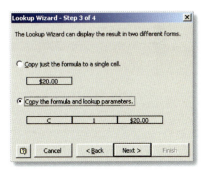

Step 5: In the last step, type or select a cell where you want to copy the lookup formula, and then click **Finish**.

Summary

The key points discussed in this lesson are:

- ◆ In Excel 2003, you can add a named range.
- ◆ You can use a named range in a formula to simplify the process of creating a formula.
- ◆ Excel allows you to use the **HLOOKUP** and **VLOOKUP** functions to locate a specific value from within a table or array.

Importing and Exporting Data

One of Excel's convenient features is the ability to import and export data. Rather than having to retype or copy and paste information, Excel provides you with easy-to-use importing and exporting tools.

Objectives

Upon completing this lesson, you will be able to:

- ✔ Import data from text files

- ✔ Import data from Microsoft Word using drag and drop

- ✔ Import a table from an HTML file

- ✔ Export data to other applications

Importing Data from Text Files

Importing data from a text file into Excel can make the data easier to read and manage.

To import data from a text file:

Step 1: Select **Data > Import External Data > Import Data….**

Step 2: In the **Import Text File** dialog box, select the text file to import and click **Import.**

Step 3: The Text Import Wizard dialog box appears. This wizard contains three steps. The wizard will analyse your imported data and make a determination as to what kind of data is being imported. The options are **Delimited** and **Fixed width:.**

Step 4: Verify that the correct data type is selected.

Step 5: Verify that the **number 1** is displayed in the **Start import at row:** field.

Step 6: Click **Next.**

Step 7: Verify that the **Tab** box is selected in the **Delimiters** section.

Step 8: Click **Next**.

Step 9: Verify that **General** is selected in the **Column data format** section.

Step 10: In the **Data preview** section, verify that the word **General** is displayed in all the column headings.

Step 11: Click **Finish.**

Step 12: The Import Data dialog box will appear.

Step 13: Select **New Worksheet** as the location where your imported data is displayed and then click **OK.**

Importing Data from Microsoft Word using Drag and Drop

Importing data using drag and drop is an easy method of exchanging information between Microsoft Office software programs.

To import data from Microsoft Word to Microsoft Excel using drag and drop:

Step 1: Open a Microsoft Word document that already contains data.

Step 2: Open a blank Excel worksheet.

Step 3: Size the Excel application window and the Word application window so that both of them are visible.

Step 4: In the Word document, highlight the text to drag and drop into the Excel spreadsheet.

Step 5: Right-click and hold onto the highlighted text.

Step 6: Drag the highlighted text onto the worksheet and release the mouse button. The Shortcut menu appears. The options are:

- **Move Here**: removes the text from the first document and places it in the worksheet.

- **Copy Here**: copies the text from the first document and inserts it into the worksheet.

- **Copy Here as Document**: places the text into the worksheet as a Word document.

- **Link Document Here**: inserts the text and makes the text a hyperlink that returns to the original document.

- **Create Hyperlink Here**: inserts the text into a single cell and makes the copied text a hyperlink that returns to the original document.

- **Create Shortcut Here**: places a Microsoft Word icon in your spreadsheet. When the icon is double-clicked, a new Word document opens that contains the highlighted text.

Step 7: Select **Copy Here.**

Importing a Table from an HTML File

To import data from an HTML file:

Step 1: In the worksheet, select the cell that will become the upper-left cell in the imported table.

Step 2: Select **Data > Import External Data > New Web Query**. The New Web Query dialog box opens. Follow the three steps to import a table from an HTML file.

Step 3: Enter an Internet address that contains a table. If you do not already have a Web site identified, click **Browse** and browse the Web.

Step 4: Select whether to import: the entire page, only the tables, or one or more specific tables. If you choose to import a specific table, you must know the name of the table and enter it into the appropriate text field.

Step 5: Select how much formatting you would like to keep from the Web page: None, Rich Text Formatting Only, or Full HTML Formatting.

Step 6: Click **OK**.

The table is imported into your worksheet. Often, the table will need additional formatting after it has been imported into your worksheet.

To import data from an HTML file using drag and drop:

Step 1: Open the Web page that contains the table to import into your worksheet.

Step 2: Make sure you are viewing the worksheet where you wish to insert the table.

Step 3: Size the Web page window and the Excel window so that both of them are visible.

Step 4: Highlight the table in the Web page.

Step 5: Click and drag the table into the range of cells on your worksheet where you would like the table to reside.

Step 6: Release your mouse button.

Round Tripping

Round-tripping HTML documents makes it easy to edit HTML files by simply selecting **File > Edit with Microsoft Excel** while in Internet Explorer. This will round-trip the document back into its native Office file format for further editing.

To round-trip an Excel worksheet:

Step 1: Open the workbook you want to publish to the Internet.

Step 2: Select **File > Save as Web Page…**.

Step 3: Name the workbook and select the **Save in**: location.

Step 4: Using the protocol set forth at your company, publish the workbook to a Web site.

Step 5: After the workbook is published, open your Web browser and view the workbook.

Step 6: Select **File > Edit with Microsoft Excel**. The original Excel workbook will open. Make the necessary changes to the workbook.

Step 7: When you have completed all of your changes, select **File > Save as Web Page…** and republish the workbook.

Exporting Data to Other Applications

Exporting data from an Excel worksheet into Microsoft Word not only saves time, but also eliminates the chances of missing a particular section of the worksheet in the Word document.

To insert a workbook into a Word file:

Step 1: Open the Word document in which the workbook is to be inserted.

Step 2: From the Menu bar in the Word document, select **Insert > File…**. The Insert File dialog box appears.

Step 3: In the Insert file dialog box, select the file type: **All Files**.

Step 4: From the **Look In:** drop-down list, locate the workbook file you wish to import into your Word document. Click the file and then click **Insert**. The **Open Worksheet** dialog box appears.

Step 5: In the **Open Document in Workbook** drop-down list, select whether you want to import the entire workbook or just a single worksheet and then click **OK**.

Summary

The key points discussed in this lesson are:

◆ Excel 2003 allows you to import data from text files.

◆ You can easily import data from Microsoft Word using drag and drop.

◆ You can import a table from an HTML file.

◆ Excel also allows you to export data to other applications.

Formatting Numbers

Excel comes equipped with a wide variety of formatting options. In this lesson, you will learn how to apply existing formats and also how to create your own.

Objectives

Upon completing this lesson, you will be able to:

✔ Apply number formats

✔ Create customer number formats

✔ Create conditional formatting

Applying Number Formats

Using number formats allows you to quickly enter unformatted numbers and apply a specific format to any number of cells at one time.

To apply number formats:

Step 1: Select the cells you want to format.

Step 2: Select **Format > Cells...**. The Format Cells dialog box appears.

Step 3: Click the **Number** tab.

Step 4: In the **Category:** section, select the desired format option. Some formats have additional options to choose from; for example, Currency has options for decimal places, symbols, and negative numbers.

Step 5: Click **OK.**

Creating Custom Number Formats

Using code, you can create custom number formats that are not included in Excel.

Code	Use	Example
" "	Indicates a text string	###"/per hour" formats 125 as 125/per hour.
( )	Formats negative numbers	(##,###) formats −87664 as (87,654)
#	Displays only significant digits	###.## formats 7.20 as 7.2 and 6.517 as 6.52
0	Displays all digits; placeholders on the right side of the decimal point are filled with trailing zeros, if necessary	##0.00 formats 4.6 as 4.60
?	Aligns decimal or slash placeholders and displays significant digits	???.?? aligns decimals and displays 6.50 as 6.5 and 8.89 as 8.9
/	Displays numbers as fractions.	# ??/?? displays 9.25 as 9 1/4
,	Thousands separator; this code is also used to format numbers as if they were divided by a thousand or a million	##,### displays 55555 as 55,555
-	Places a hyphen in a number	000-000 formats 345678 as 345-678

To create a custom number format:

Step 1: Select the cells to format.

Step 2: Select **Format > Cells...**. The Format Cells dialog box appears.

Step 3: In the **Category:** section, select **Custom**.

Step 4: In the **Type:** section, single-click each option to view how the numbers will look in the Sample section.

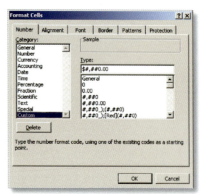

Step 5: In the **Type:** text field, type an example from the Number Format Codes table to preview how your numbers will look.

Step 6: Select the Custom Number Format to use, and click **OK**.

Using Conditional Formatting

Conditional formatting allows you to apply formats to selected cells based on a condition you create. A condition is an expression that is either true or false. For example, if an employee raised more than £500 for charity this year, that employee would receive a gift certificate.

To create conditional formatting:

Step 1: Select the cells that contain the numeric values.

Step 2: Select **Format > Conditional Formatting…**. The Conditional Formatting dialog box displays.

Step 3: Using the first drop-down list, select whether the condition applies to a Cell Value or a Formula.

Step 4: In the second drop-down list, select whether the value is to be:

- Between
- Not between
- Equal to
- Not equal to
- Greater than
- Less than
- Greater than or equal to
- Less than or equal to

Step 5: In the **Condition** text box, type a constant, a formula, or a cell in the worksheet.

Step 6: Click the **Format** button to format the cell by selecting font, border, or fill characteristics. Then click **OK** to close the Formatting dialog box.

Step 7: Click **OK** to close the Conditional Formatting dialog box.

Building on the example used earlier, if the employee raised more than £3500, that employee would receive a car. Use the same conditional formatting you created before to add an additional condition. Use the following graphic as a guideline:

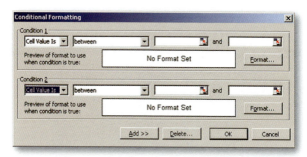

To add additional conditions based on the previous example:

Step 1: Select the cells to format.

Step 2: Select **Format > Conditional Formatting.** The Conditional Formatting dialog box appears.

Step 3: Using the first drop-down list, select whether the condition applies to a Cell Value or a Formula.

Step 4: In the second drop-down list, select between.

Step 5: In the first condition text box, type **500.**

Step 6: In the second condition text box, type **3499**.

Step 7: Click the **Add** button to add the additional condition. The Conditional Formatting dialog box adds another condition.

Step 8: Select whether the condition applies to a Cell Value or a Formula.

Step 9: In the second drop-down list, select **Greater Than**.

Step 10: In the condition text box, type **3500**.

Step 11: Click the **Format** button to format what the cell will look like. Select font, border, and fill characteristics, and then click **OK** to close the Formatting dialog box.

Step 12: Click **OK** to close the Conditional Formatting dialog box.

To delete a condition:

Step 1: Select **Format > Conditional Formatting**. The Conditional Formatting dialog box appears.

Step 2: Click the **Delete** button.

Step 3: Select the condition(s) to delete.

Step 4: Click **OK**.

Step 5: Click **OK** again to close the Conditional Formatting dialog box.

Summary

The key points discussed in this lesson are:

◆ You can apply number formats and a specific format to any number of cells at one time.

◆ Excel allows you to create custom number formats.

◆ You can also use conditional formatting to apply formats to selected cells based on a condition you create.

Collaborating with Workgroups

One of the benefits of using Excel is its ability to allow multiple users to view and modify a single workbook simultaneously. In this lesson, you will learn how to create and manage a shared workbook.

Objectives

Upon completing this lesson, you will be able to:

✔ Create, format, edit, and remove comments in your worksheets

✔ Apply and remove worksheet and workbook protection

✔ Change workbook properties

✔ Set, change, and remove file passwords

✔ Track changes to your workbook

✔ Create a shared workbook

✔ Merge workbooks

Working with Comments

Adding comments to a worksheet can provide additional information to others who view the worksheet.

To create a comment:

Step 1: Select the cell to add a comment.

Step 2: Select **Insert > Comment**. A text box appears.

Step 3: Type a comment into the text box.

Step 4: Click any other cell in your workbook to close the text box.

Step 5: A red triangle appears in the upper-right corner of the cell that contains the comment.

Step 6: To view the comment, hover the mouse over the cell that contains the comment.

To edit and format a comment:

Step 1: Right-click the cell containing the comment to change.

Step 2: From the **Shortcut menu**, select **Edit Comment**.

Step 3: Highlight the text to format. From the **Formatting** toolbar, change the font format.

Step 4: If needed, retype any text that needs to be changed.

Step 5: Click the text box border to format the fill and line colour. Select fill and line colours and options.

Step 6: Click any other cell in the workbook to close the text box.

Step 7: To view the formatted comment, hover your mouse over the cell that contains the comment.

To delete a comment:

Step 1: Right-click the cell containing the comment to delete.

Step 2: From the **Shortcut** menu, select **Delete Comment**.

Applying and Removing Worksheet and Workbook Protection

Using protection in your workbook can ensure that protected data is not compromised in any way.

To apply protection to a worksheet:

Step 1: Select **Tools > Protection > Protect Sheet...**. The Protect Sheet dialog box appears.

Step 2: In the **Allow all users of this worksheet to:** section, select the actions that you would like to allow all users to be able to perform, and deselect any actions that you want to prevent users from performing.

Step 3: If you want to make the sheet password protected, type a password into the **Password to unprotect sheet:** text field.

Step 4: Retype the password in the **Confirm Password** dialog box.

Step 5: Click **OK**.

To apply protection to a workbook:

Step 1: Select **Tools > Protection > Protect Workbook**. The Protect Workbook dialog box appears.

Step 2: In the **Protect workbook for** section, choose the components of the workbook to be protected.

Step 3: If you want to make the workbook password protected, type a password into the **Password** text field.

Step 4: Retype the password in the **Confirm Password** dialog box.

Step 5: Click **OK**.

 Note - There is no way to recover a protection password. Make sure to write down your password and keep it stored somewhere safe.

To remove protection from a workbook or worksheet:

Step 1: Select **Tools > Protection > Unprotect Workbook...** or **Tools > Protection > Unprotect Sheet...**.

Step 2: If you created a protection password, a dialog box will prompt you to enter the password. Enter the password and click **OK.**

Setting, Changing, and Removing File Passwords

Creating a file password restricts who can view or modify information in your workbook.

To set a file password:

Step 1: Select **File > Save As**. The Save As dialog box appears.

Step 2: In the upper-right corner of the Save As dialog box, click **Tools**, and select **General Options...**. The Save Options dialog box appears.

Step 3: In the **Save Options** dialog box, select the options you wish to engage, or type the password that corresponds with the type of protection you want to add to the workbook.

Step 4: When you enter a password and click **OK**, the **Confirm Password** dialog box appears. Retype your password and click **OK**.

Step 5: In the **Save As** dialog box, click **Save**.

To delete a file password:

Step 1: Select **File > Save As**. The Save As dialog box appears.

Step 2: In the upper-right corner of the **Save As** dialog box, click **Tools**, and select **General Options**. The Save Options dialog box appears.

Step 3: In the **Save Options** dialog box, highlight the asterisks that represent the password you previously entered and press **Delete**. Next, click **OK**.

Step 4: In the **Save As** dialog box, click **Save** or **Cancel**.

To change a file password:

Step 1: Select **File > Save As**. The Save As dialog box appears.

Step 2: In the upper-right corner of the **Save As** dialog box, click **Tools**, and select **General Options**. The Save Options dialog box appears.

Step 3: In the **Save Options** dialog box, highlight the asterisks that represent the password you previously entered and type the new password.

Step 4: When you enter a new password, the **Confirm Password** dialog box appears. Retype your new password and click **OK**.

Step 5: In the **Save As** dialog box, click **Save**.

Changing Workbook Properties

Changing workbook properties allows you to easily organise and locate specific workbooks.

To access workbook properties:

Step 1: While in an open workbook, select **File > Properties**. The Properties dialog box appears. There are five tabs in the Properties dialog box:

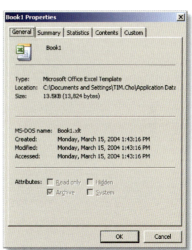

- **General:** displays the attributes of the file.

- **Summary:** displays information including author, subject, title, company, and keywords, and it is editable.

- **Statistics:** displays when the file was modified, accessed, created, or printed; by whom it was last saved; its revision number; and the total editing time.

- **Contents:** displays the name of each sheet in the workbook and the workbook itself.

- **Custom:** allows you to enter information relating to different properties including editor, owner, date completed, purpose, received from, telephone number, and typist, and it is editable.

Step 2: Click the **Summary** tab and enter the appropriate information into each text field.

Step 3: Click **OK**.

 Note - Make sure that the workbook is not protected. You will need to remove workbook protection to access its properties.

Tracking Changes

When working with a shared workbook, it is often convenient to see the changes that are being made by other users. After you activate Track Changes, every changed cell is noted with a comment. Simply roll the mouse over the comment to view details on the change, such as who changed it, when it was changed, and the previous value in the cell.

To enable Track Changes:

    Step 1: Select **Tools > Track Changes > Highlight Changes...**.

    Step 2: Click the box next to **Track changes while editing**.

    Step 3: Select which changes you want highlighted, and then click **OK**.

Creating a Shared Workbook

A shared workbook allows more than one user to open and modify the workbook at the same time.

To create a shared workbook:

Step 1: Select **Tools > Share Workbook...**. The Share Workbook dialog box appears.

Step 2: Click the **Editing** tab.

Step 3: Select the **Allow Changes...** option.

Step 4: Click the **Advanced** tab.

Step 5: Select the options you wish to associate with the workbook, and then click **OK**.

Merging Workbooks

Merging workbooks is an easy way to review and update changes made to a shared workbook.

To merge workbooks:

Step 1: Open a copy of the workbook.

Step 2: From the **Tools** menu, select **Compare and Merge Workbooks**.... The Select Files to Merge Into Current Workbook dialog box appears.

Step 3: Select the copy of the shared workbook that you want to merge, and then click **OK**.

 Note - To select multiple workbooks, hold down the **Ctrl** or **Shift** keys while selecting the workbooks you would like to merge.

Summary

The key points discussed in this lesson are:

◆ Excel allows you to use comments to clarify information found in your workbook.

◆ You can protect the contents of your workbooks by applying protection or using a password.

◆ Excel allows you to change workbook properties.

◆ You can track changes in a workbook so that you are always aware of modifications to its content.

◆ You can easily create a shared workbook so that others may modify and update workbook information.

◆ Excel allows you to merge shared workbooks together so that the latest content is upgraded into your workbook.

Module 4: Advanced Excel Features

This module will teach you about advanced Excel features. You will learn how to create workbooks that showcase the most important parts of your data, solve problems, and automate commonly used tasks.

Objectives

Upon completing this module, you will be able to:

- ✔ Audit a worksheet
- ✔ Display and format data
- ✔ Use analysis tools
- ✔ Use macros
- ✔ Use multiple workbooks

Outline

This module contains these lessons:

- ➤ Auditing a Worksheet
- ➤ Displaying and Formatting Data
- ➤ Using Analysis Tools
- ➤ Using Macros
- ➤ Using Multiple Workbooks

Auditing a Worksheet

Excel provides a number of tools designed to audit the formulas in worksheets. Auditing tools such as tracing precedents and dependents allow you to view the relationship of cell references in your formula. These tools enable you to understand the structure of your formulas and models.

Objectives

Upon completing this lesson, you will be able to:

- Use the Formula Auditing toolbar
- Identify error codes
- Trace errors
- Trace precedents and dependents

The Formula Auditing Toolbar

The Formula Auditing toolbar provides quick access to commonly used auditing functions. From left to right, the buttons on the Formula Auditing toolbar are:

- Error Checking
- Trace Precedents
- Remove Precedent Arrows
- Trace Dependents
- Remove Dependent Arrows
- Remove All Arrows
- Trace Error
- New Comment
- Circle Invalid Data
- Clear Validation Circles
- Show Watch Window
- Evaluate Formula

Precedents - Cells that are referred to by a formula in another cell. For example, if cell C9 contains the formula =A3, cell A3 is a precedent to cell C9.

Dependents - Cells that contain formulas that refer to other cells. For example, if cell C9 contains the formula =A3, cell C9 is a dependent of cell A3.

Identifying Error Codes

There are eight standard error codes that can appear in a worksheet to inform you that a formula requires attention. When an error code appears, it is helpful to trace dependents or precedents so that you may easily fix the error. The eight standard error codes are:

Error Code/Error Name	Reason for Error
######	• The data does not fit into the cell • One date was subtracted from another and the result was a negative number
#DIV/0 (Division by Zero)	The number or cell reference you divided by is either blank or zero; you may need an absolute cell reference in the original formula
#N/A (Not Available)	• A required argument in a function has been omitted • The cell that contains the argument is blank or doesn't have the kind of entry the function requires
#NAME	• The name of a range or function is spelled incorrectly • There is a reference to a name that does not exist • There is text in a formula or format that does not have quotation marks • A colon was left out in a range, i.e., (H8N32) instead of: (H8:N32)
#NULL	You referred to an intersection that doesn't exist by using a space between two ranges in an argument
#NUM	• There is text or a blank cell in an argument that requires a number • There is a formula that creates a number too large or too small for Excel to handle
#REF (Invalid Reference)	Required cells in a formula have been deleted, so the formula cannot find the cell that it refers to

Tracing Errors

Excel also provides an auditing tool for tracing error values in a formula. It works like the other auditing tools by displaying a number of arrows highlighting the cells in your worksheet that are used in a particular calculation. The Error Tracer displays only those components of the formula that contain error values. The tool will also trace backward to activate the original cell that is causing the error.

To trace errors:

Step 1: Select a cell within an error.

Step 2: On the Auditing toolbar, click **Trace Error**.

Step 3: The lines that appear will guide you to the cells that contain the error.

Step 4: Fix the error.

Step 5: On the Auditing Toolbar, click **Remove All Arrows**.

In the example, the Trace Errors command drew a line that pointed to the cells that make up the formula in cell F3. To fix this example, you would select cell B3, enter a numeric value and press Enter.

Tracing Precedents and Dependents

Tracing precedents and dependents allows you to see the relationship of cell references in your formula and how they work together.

To trace a precedent:

Step 1: Select **View > Toolbars > Formula Auditing** to view the Formula Auditing toolbar. If the Formula Auditing toolbar is not visible in the Toolbars list, you may need to select **View > Toolbars > Customise** and from the Toolbars tab, select **Formula Auditing**, and then click **Close**.

Step 2: Click a cell that contains a formula.

Step 3: On the **Formula Auditing** toolbar, click **Trace Precedents**. A number of lines and arrows will be added to your worksheet to show you which cells have precedent on the selected formula.

Step 4: Each time you click the **Trace Precedents** button, Excel will move into deeper levels of the formula.

In the example, two precedents were drawn. One from cell J14 to cell N3 and another from cell N3 to cell range B3:M3. This means that the formula in cell J14 uses information from cell N3 to formulate its value and that the formula in cell N3 uses the cell range B3:M3 to formulate its value. In this example, the precedent cell for cell J17 is N3 and the precedent cells for cell N3 is the cell range B3:M3.

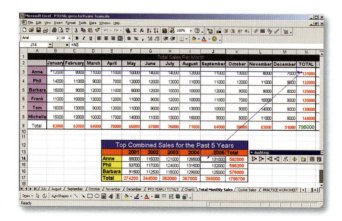

To trace a dependent:

Step 1: Select **View > Toolbars > Formula Auditing** to view the Formula Auditing toolbar. If the Formula Auditing toolbar is not visible in the Toolbars list, you may need to select **View > Toolbars > Customise** and from the **Toolbars** tab, select **Formula Auditing**, and then click **Close**.

Step 2: Click a cell that contains a formula.

Step 3: On the **Formula Auditing** toolbar, click **Trace Dependents**. A number of lines and arrows will be added to your worksheet to show you which cells are dependent on the selected formula.

Step 4: Each time you click the **Trace Dependents** button, Excel will move into deeper levels of the formula.

In the example, dependents were drawn from cell J14 to cell K14 and cell J17. This means that cells K14 and J17 use information from cell J14 to formulate their value. In this example, the dependent cells are K14 and J17. They depend on cell J14 to provide them with information.

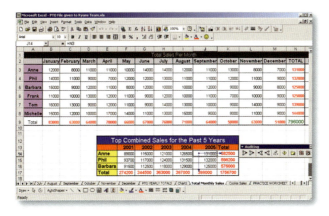

To remove a trace, on the **Formula Auditing** toolbar click either the **Remove Precedent Arrows** or the **Remove Dependent Arrows** button.

Summary

The key points discussed in this lesson are:

◆ The Formula Auditing Toolbar is a helpful tool in Excel.

◆ Excel makes it easy for you to identify and understand error codes.

◆ Excel allows you to trace errors, including tracing precedents and dependents in the event of an error.

Displaying and Formatting Data

In this lesson, you will learn several techniques for displaying and formatting your data in multiple ways, depending upon your ultimate objective.

Objectives

Upon completing this lesson, you will be able to:

- Perform single and multilevel sorts
- Use subtotalling
- Use data forms
- Use grouping and outlines
- Apply data filters
- Extract data
- Query databases
- Use data validation

Performing Single and Multilayer Sorts

Performing a sort allows you to easily organise or alphabetise a worksheet. When you select the first cell in the range to sort, Excel automatically includes all cells above, below, to the right, and left of the selected cell until it reaches an empty row or column.

To sort information in a worksheet:

Step 1: Select either the first cell in the range you want sorted or the entire worksheet.

Step 2: Select **Data > Sort...**. The Sort dialog box appears.

Step 3: Select the column to sort by first, and then select whether to sort ascending or descending.

Step 4: To perform a multi-layer sort, select another condition from the **Then by** drop-down list(s).

Step 5: In the **My data range has** section, select whether or not the selected cells contain a header row and then click **OK** to sort the data.

Note - If you select a column or row instead of the first cell in the range or the entire worksheet, the Sort Warning dialog box appears and tells you that Excel will sort only the column(s) or row(s) you have selected. Select how you would like to proceed, and then click either **Sort...** or **Cancel**.

Using Subtotalling

The term subtotalling is often regarded as the sum of a specific number of variables. With Excel, subtotalling can refer to average, count, minimum, maximum, or another statistical calculation based on a group of cells.

To subtotal a section of a workbook:

Step 1: Sort the records in the field to be subtotalled.

Step 2: Select any cell in the area to subtotal.

Step 3: Select **Data > Subtotals…**.

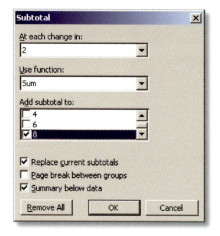

Step 4: In the **At each change in:** drop-down list, select the sorted field.

Step 5: From the **Use function:** drop-down list, select a type of subtotal.

Step 6: Select the numeric fields to be subtotalled when the value of the **At each change in:** field changes and then click **OK**.

Using Data Forms

Data forms allow you to enter or search for data in a non-cell environment. Cells that do not contain formulas appear in an editable format, whereas cells that do contain formulas are visible, but are not available to edit.

To open a data form:

Step 1: Select the cells you want to create a data form for and select **Data > Form**.... A dialog box appears.

Step 2: Excel uses the column headers in your cell range as the field names. The values contained within your cells can be edited in the text box to the right of the field name.

Step 3: Use the vertical scroll bar or the **Find Prev/Find Next** buttons to navigate through each section of the selected cells.

Step 4: To add a new record, click **New.** The new record appears at the end of your selected cell range.

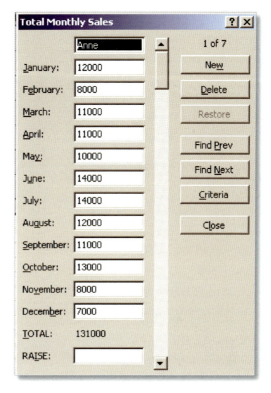

Step 5: To delete a record, make sure you are viewing the record you want to delete, and then click **Delete.** A dialog box will open asking if you want to delete the record permanently. Click either **OK** or **Cancel**.

Using Grouping and Outlines

Grouping worksheets together ensures that any changes made or formatting applied to one sheet will be applied to the remainder of the sheets in the group.

To group worksheets:

Step 1: Hold the **Ctrl** key and click the sheet tabs of each worksheet you would like to add to a group.

Step 2: All sheet tabs that are in a group will be white.

To ungroup worksheets:

Step 1: Hold the **Ctrl** key and click the sheet tabs of each worksheet you would like to remove from a group.

Step 2: The tabs of the removed sheets will return to their normal colour.

Adding outlines to a workbook allows you to easily read worksheets that contain multiple levels of detail.

- To add an outline using a worksheet that contains at least one formula, select **Data > Group and Outline > Auto Outline.**
- To remove an outline, **Select Data > Group and Outline > Clear Outline.**

To use an outline:

Step 1: When you initially add an outline, all of the cells that contain data are visible. Click the minus sign to hide precedent cells.

Step 2: To unhide precedent cells, click the plus sign.

Applying Data Filters

Applying data filters allows you to select all of the cells that meet a certain requirement and temporarily hide all of the other cells in your worksheet.

To apply a filter:

Step 1: Select a cell, specific columns, or rows to which you would like to apply a filter.

Step 2: Select **Data > Filter > AutoFilter.** A drop-down arrow appears next to each field name.

Step 3: The drop-down list will list each cell name and the following selections:

	A	B	C	D	E
			Cookie Sales!		
1					
2		Chocolate chi	Oatme	Suga	Peanut butte
3	(All)	6	2	4	7
4	(Top 10...)	4	7	9	2
5	(Custom...) April	3	3	2	6
6	August December	4	2	9	7
7	February January	6	5	6	10
8	July June	5	7	8	6
9	March May	4	6	9	7
10	November October	9	4	1	4
11	September Total:	7	6	2	7
12	October	8	9	4	5
13	November	11	2	2	11
14	December	14	11	9	12
15	Total:	81	64	65	84

- (All) - The entire list of fields in the column

- (Top 10) - Used in numeric fields to show the top or bottom ten, or any other number that you specify

- (Custom) - Allows you to create a custom filter

- (Blanks) - Blank cells

- (NonBlanks) - Cells that are not blank

Note - The (Blanks) and (NonBlanks) selections are available only if the column you want to filter contains a blank cell.

Step 4: Select the filter from the drop-down list. The cells (records) that do not contain the specified information will be hidden.

Step 5: The row numbers of filtered records appear in blue. The drop-down arrow of any column being actively filtered also turns blue.

To create a custom filter:

Step 1: Apply an AutoFilter to the selected cells.

Step 2: From the **Filter** drop-down list, select **Custom**. The Custom AutoFilter dialog box appears.

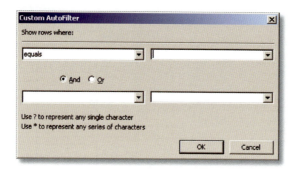

Step 3: You can set the parameters of the filter. The two drop-down lists on the left side of the Custom AutoFilter dialog box allow you to select an operator. The two drop-down lists on the right side of the Custom AutoFilter dialog box allow you to select the values represented in the selected cells. Make the operator and value selections.

Step 4: Select **And** for a range, or select **Or** to filter for more than one possible value, and then click **OK**.

 Note - If you print your worksheet when it is filtered, only the filtered records will print.

Extracting Data Using an Advanced Filter

To extract data using an Advanced Filter:

Step 1: Copy the column labels in the worksheet to a new worksheet.

Step 2: Enter the criteria for the filter directly under the column labels in the new worksheet.

Step 3: Click any cell in the range in the original worksheet. Excel will automatically select the entire range that is bound by a blank column and row. Or, select only the range of cells you want to filter.

Step 4: Select **Data > Filter > Advanced Filter…**. The Advanced Filter dialog box opens. The range or the selected cells from your original worksheet are listed in the List range: field. To select the Criteria range:, click the collapse dialog button and select the filter criteria from your new worksheet. Click the collapse dialog button again to return to the Advanced Filter dialog box.

Step 5: Select either **Filter the list, in-place** or **Copy to another location**. If you select **Copy to another location**, the Copy to: field opens. Click the collapse dialog button and select where you want the filtered information to copy.

Step 6: Click the **Unique records only** check box to display only the unique records.

Step 7: Click **OK** to run the filter.

Querying Databases

To query a database:

Step 1: Select **Data > Import External Data > New Database Query**. The Choose Data Source dialog box appears.

Step 2: On the **Databases** tab, select the type of database to use for the data source and click **OK**. The Select Database dialog box appears.

Step 3: In the **Directories:** section, locate the folder that contains the database to query.

Step 4: In the **Database Name** section, select the database to query and click **OK**. The Query Wizard appears.

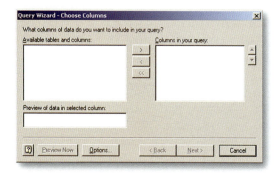

Step 5: In the **Available tables and columns:** section, select the fields to query. To view all available fields, click the plus sign next to the table name.

Step 6: Click the forward arrow button on each column to add it to the query.

Step 7: If a particular column needs to be removed, click the back arrow button.

Step 8: After all of the columns have been selected for the query, re-order them by clicking once on the column to move it and then by clicking the up/down button until the column is properly located.

Step 9: Click **Options** to select additional features for your query.

Step 10: Click **Next**.

Step 11: To filter data, click the column to filter, select the desired And/Or options, and then click **Next**. If the data will not be filtered, simply click **Next**.

Step 12: To sort data, click the drop-down arrow next to the **Sort by** text field, and select the sort options. Continue to sort the data by using the drop-down arrow next to the **Then by** text fields. Click **Next** after sorting. If the data does not need to be sorted, simply click **Next**.

Step 13: In the last step of the Query, click the radio button next to your choice of what to do next (often this will be **Return Data to Microsoft Office Excel**).

Step 14: To save the query, click **Save Query**. Name the query and select a save location. Click **Save**.

Step 15: Click **Finish**. The Excel workbook becomes active and the Import Data dialog box appears.

Step 16: Select where to enter your query and click **OK**.

Using Data Validation

Data validation allows you to set parameters in a workbook that reflect company policies and procedures. For example, to make sure all new employees are at least 16 years of age, set a data validation to display an error message if a date of birth before a certain year is entered.

The Data Validation dialog box contains three tabs:

Settings – The business rule is entered here using the parameters specific to the rule.

Input Message – You can enter a prompt that directs the user to enter the required information into the cell.

Error Alert – This area enables you to create your own error message in case the information entered into the cell range violates the business rule entered on the Settings tab.

To create a data validation:

Step 1: Select the range of cells that apply data validation settings.

Step 2: Select **Data > Validation…**. The Data Validation dialog box appears.

Step 3: In the **Allow:** drop-down list on the **Settings** tab, enter the variable for the business rule. Depending on the selection, you may need to enter additional information in the text fields.

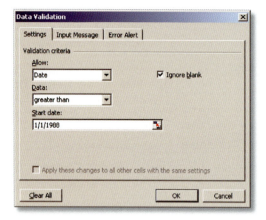

Step 4: Click the **Input Message** tab. In the **Title:** field, enter the title of the input message to appear when a user clicks on the validated cells. In the **Input message:** field, enter any additional information the user will see.

Step 5: Click the **Error Alert** tab. In the **Style:** section, select the icon to appear on the error message. In the **Title:** field, enter the title of the error message. In the **Error message:** field, enter the text for error message. Click **OK**.

Summary

The key points discussed in this lesson are:

◆ In Excel, you can perform single and multilevel sorts.

◆ You can use subtotalling to create a statistical calculation based on a group of cells.

◆ Excel allows you to use data forms to easily enter or search for data in a non-cell environment.

◆ Use grouping and outlines to ensure that any formatting changes applied to one sheet will be applied to the remainder of the sheets in the group.

◆ Apply data filters to select all of the cells that meet a certain requirement.

◆ Excel allows you to extract data and query databases.

◆ You can use data validation to set parameters in a workbook that reflect company policies and procedures.

Using Analysis Tools

In this lesson, you will learn how to utilise Excel's advanced analysis tools to support decision-making strategies and more easily analyse the contents of a workbook.

Objectives

Upon completing this lesson, you will be able to:

- ✔ Create and edit a PivotTable
- ✔ Use Goal Seek
- ✔ Work with Scenarios
- ✔ Use Solver
- ✔ Add fields to a table using a Web browser
- ✔ Use the report manager

Creating a PivotTable Using the Wizard

PivotTables summarise large amounts of data in a small amount of space in an interactive and flexible way. You can use PivotTables to:

- Summarise data from numerous sources
- Change orientation
- Group items in specific fields
- Change the calculation for the specific field
- Format the PivotTable

To create a PivotTable using the PivotTable and PivotChart Wizard:

Step 1: Select any cell in a worksheet or the range of cells to use in your PivotTable.

Step 2: Select **Data > PivotTable and PivotChart Report...**.

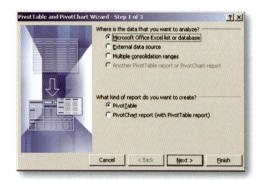

Step 3: In the **Where is the data that you want to analyse?** section, click the radio button next to your choice.

Step 4: In the **What kind of report do you want to create?** section, click the radio button next to **PivotTable**. Click **Next** to continue to Step 2 of the Wizard.

Step 5: Next, Excel autofills the range containing the cell initially selected before beginning the PivotTable Wizard if the data contained within the worksheet is being analysed. If Excel has not autofilled the correct range of cells, click the collapse dialog button and select the correct range of cells. Click **Next**.

Step 6: In Step 3 of the Wizard, the **Where do you want to put the PivotTable report?** section allows you to select whether you want the

PivotTable in a new sheet or as a part of an existing sheet. If you select the existing sheet, click the collapse dialog button and select the location where you want the PivotTable to appear.

Step 7: Click the **Layout** button to arrange the data displayed in the PivotTable. The fields from the selected data appear on the right side of the Layout dialog box.

Step 8: Select the field, drag and drop it into the section of the dialog box to create the desired layout, and then click **OK**.

Step 9: Click the **Options...** button to adjust the options for the PivotTable, and then click **OK**.

Step 10: Click **Finish** to insert the PivotTable into the workbook.

Using the Microsoft PivotTable AutoFormat

In some cases, PivotTables can be difficult to format, so Excel 2003 allows you to manipulate and format the PivotTable in the same manner as formatting the worksheet.

To AutoFormat a PivotTable:

Step 1: Select the range of cells to use to create your PivotTable.

Step 2: On the PivotTable toolbar, click the **Format Report** button.

Step 3: Select the table style from the **AutoFormat** dialog box and click **OK**.

Creating Microsoft PivotChart Reports

Creating a PivotChart to accompany a PivotTable is a great way to display information in a clear and concise format. PivotCharts default to a column chart, but you can reformat them to any type of chart other than bubble, stock or scatter charts.

To create a PivotChart report using the PivotTable and PivotChart Wizard:

Step 1: Select either a cell in the worksheet or the range of cells to use in your PivotChart.

Step 2: Select **Data > PivotTable and PivotChart Report…**. The PivotTable and PivotChart Wizard appears. There are three steps in the Wizard.

Step 3: In Step 1 of the Wizard, click the radio button next to your choice in the **Where is the data that you want to analyse?** section.

Step 4: In the **What kind of report do you want to create?** section, click the radio button next to **PivotChart report (with PivotTable report)**.

Step 5: In Step 2 of the Wizard, Excel autofills the range containing the cell initially selected before beginning the Wizard, if the data contained the worksheet is being analysed. If Excel has not correctly autofilled the range, or the range needs to be changed, click the collapse dialog button and select the correct range of cells. Click **Next**.

Step 6: In Step 3 of the Wizard, select whether you want the PivotTable and the PivotChart to each appear in a new sheet or as a part of an existing sheet in the **Where do you want to put the PivotTable report?** section. If existing sheet is selected, click the collapse dialog button and select the location where the PivotTable is to appear. The PivotChart will always appear on its own new sheet.

Step 7: Click the **Layout** button to arrange the data displayed in the PivotTable. The fields from the selected data appear on the right side of the Layout dialog box.

Step 8: Select the field, and drag and drop it into the section of the dialog box to create the desired layout. Click **OK**.

Step 9: Click the **Options** button to adjust the options for PivotTable and PivotChart, and then click **OK**.

Step 10: Click **Finish** to insert the PivotTable and PivotChart into the workbook.

To create a PivotChart from an existing PivotTable:

Step 1: Click any cell in the PivotTable.

Step 2: From the **PivotTable** toolbar, click the **Chart Wizard** button. A PivotChart will be inserted into a new sheet.

Using Goal Seek

Goal Seek is a feature of Excel that is used to make calculations backwards. Goal Seek determines the values necessary to achieve a specific goal. For example, if you need to make £250,000 on the sale of a new product, Goal Seek will determine how many units of that product must be sold to achieve your £250,000 target.

To use Goal Seek:

Step 1: Select **Tools > Goal Seek…**. The Goal Seek dialog box appears.

Step 2: Use the collapse dialog button and select a set cell. This cell is where the goal value will appear and must contain a formula.

Step 3: In the **To value:** text field, enter the goal value.

Step 4: In the **By changing cell:** text field, enter the value to change, and then click **OK** to start Goal Seek.

Step 5: Click **OK** in the **Goal Seek** Status dialog box to accept the solution. Click **Cancel** to reject the solution.

Working with Scenarios

Using Excel's Scenarios feature, you can create and save different groups of values, and then view the results of different scenarios with just a few clicks of the mouse. This feature is valuable when trying to simulate worst case or best case scenarios.

To create and display multiple scenarios:

Step 1: Select **Tools > Scenarios...**. The Scenario Manager appears.

Step 2: To create a scenario, click **Add...**.

Step 3: In the **Scenario name:** field, type a name for the scenario.

Step 4: In the **Changing cells:** field, enter references for the cells that need to change. If desired, enable protection options and then click **OK**. The Scenario Values dialog box appears.

Step 5: Enter the values you want for the changing cells. Click **OK** to finish creating the scenario.

Step 6: Click **Add...** to create additional scenarios and repeat the steps listed above.

Step 7: To view one of your scenarios, choose it from the list in the Scenario Manager dialog box, and then click **Show**.

Using Solver

Solver is another forecasting tool in Excel, and is used to find the optimal solution to a problem or question.

To use Solver:

Step 1: Select **Tools > Solver**. The Solver Parameters dialog box appears.

Step 2: In the Set **Target Cell:** field, click the collapse dialog button and select a target cell.

Step 3: Choose an **Equal To:** option.

Step 4: In the **By Changing Cells:** text field, enter the cell to be changed and then click **Solve**.

Step 5: To replace the original values select **Keep Solver Solution**. To discard the solution, select **Restore Original Values**. Click **OK**.

Creating Interactive Tables for the Web with PivotTable

To create an interactive table for the Web with PivotTable:

Step 1: Select the part of the workbook to publish to the Web.

Step 2: Select **File > Save as Web Page….** The Save As dialog box appears.

Step 3: In the **Save** section, select either the entire workbook or sheet.

Step 4: Click the check box next to **Add interactivity**.

Step 5: Click **Publish…**. The Publish as Web Page dialog box appears.

Step 6: In the **Items to publish section**, select the item to publish from the **Choose:** drop-down list.

Step 7: In the **Viewing options** section, select a type of functionality from the **Add interactivity with:** drop-down list.

Step 8: In the **Publish as** section, click the **Change…** button to change the title that will appear in the title bar of the browser window.

Step 9: Enter a file name and location, or click **Browse…** to select a file name and location for the Web page.

Step 10: Leave the **Open published web page in browser** check box enabled to preview the completed page. Click **Publish** to create the interactive Web page.

Adding Fields to a Table Using the Web Browser

To add fields to a table using the Web browser:

Step 1: While in Internet Explorer, open the PivotTable page.

Step 2: On the toolbar, click the **Field List** button to open the Field List.

Step 3: Select the field you want to add to the PivotTable list.

Step 4: Drag and drop the field in the PivotTable list, or select the field in the Field List.

Step 5: In the drop-down list, choose the area where you want to place the field and click **Add to** to place the field in the drop area.

Using the Report Manager

The Report Manager creates reports that can include scenarios and views. If the Report Manager does not appear in the View menu, select **Tools > Add-Ins…**. In the Add-Ins dialog box, place a check mark next to Report Manager and then click **OK**.

To create a new report:

Step 1: Select **View > Report Manager**. The Report Manager dialog appears.

Step 2: Click **Add**. The Add Report dialog box appears.

Step 3: In the **Report Name** text field, enter a report name.

Step 4: In **Section to Add**, select a sheet to add to the report. You can also add a view or scenario to the report by clicking the check boxes next to View and/or Scenario and then selecting the view or scenario you wish to include.

Step 5: Click **Add** to add the section to the report.

Step 6: Repeat steps 4 and 5 until all the sheets are added.

Step 7: To rearrange the report sections use the Move Up/Move Down arrows.

Step 8: To delete a section, click the **Delete** button.

Step 9: To print the report with page numbers, click the check box next to **Use Continuous Page Numbers**.

Step 10: To add the report to the Report Manager, click **OK**.

Step 11: Click **OK** again to close the Report Manger dialog box.

Summary

The key points discussed in this lesson are:

◆ Excel allows you to create and edit a PivotTable so that you can easily manage information in your workbook.

◆ You can use Goal Seek to calculate backwards.

◆ Work with Scenarios to create and save different groups of values and then view their results.

◆ Use Solver to find the optimal solution to a problem or question.

◆ Excel allows you to add fields to a table using a Web browser.

◆ Use the report manager to create reports.

Using Macros

Macros are a convenient way of automating commonly used tasks. Macros can be added to a toolbar, menu bar, or shortcut key.

Objectives

Upon completing this lesson, you will be able to:

- ✔ Record macros
- ✔ Run macros
- ✔ Edit macros
- ✔ Assign a macro to a command button

Recording Macros

Recording macros enable you to automate commonly used tasks. You can place a shortcut to the task on the Menu bar, on a toolbar, or as a keystroke combination. Before you record macros, it is important to know the steps. The macro recorder records each action taken, but does not record the time taken between actions, so take your time when recording macros.

It is also important to note that when recording macros, any cell clicked is recorded as an absolute reference. To make cell references of macros relative, click the **Use Relative References** button on the **Macro** recording toolbar.

To record macros:

Step 1: Select **Tools > Macro > Record New Macro…**.

Step 2: The Record Macro dialog box appears.

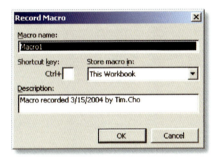

Step 3: In the **Macro name:** field, enter a name for the macro. The name can be up to 255 characters long, must begin with a letter, can have no spaces, and can contain no punctuation other than an underscore.

Step 4: In the **Description:** field, enter a description for the macro.

Step 5: Select where the Macro is to be stored. The **Store macro in:** drop-down list provides options for saving the macro. The options are **This Workbook**, **Personal Macro Workbook**, and **New Workbook**.

Step 6: The **Shortcut key:** field allows you to assign a key combination to the macro, if desired.

Step 7: Click **OK**. The Macro recording toolbar appears.

Step 8: Click the **Relative Reference** button on the **Macro recording** toolbar.

Step 9: The macro automatically begins recording. Do not push the

Record button on the **Macro recording** toolbar.

Step 10: Click through your steps to record to the macro.

Step 11: Click the **Stop Recording** button on the **Macro recording** toolbar when finished.

 Note - Keep in mind that many of the keys on the keyboard are already assigned a task. For example, **Ctrl + S** is the Save command. Be careful not to assign a key command already in use. It is safer to assign a macro to a toolbar or menu bar.

Running Macros

A macro allows you to perform many individual tasks with just the click of a button.

To run a macro:

Step 1: Click a cell in which to begin running the macro.

Step 2: Select **Tools > Macro > Macros…**.

Step 3: The Macro dialog box opens.

Step 4: Any recorded macros will be visible in the dialog box.

Step 5: Select the macro to run, and then click **Run**.

To change the macro's description or shortcut key:

Step 1: Select **Tools > Macro > Macros…**.

Step 2: The Macro dialog box will open.

Step 3: Any recorded macros will be visible in the dialog box.

Step 4: Select the macro to be updated by single-clicking it, and then click **Options…**. The Macro Options dialog box opens.

Step 5: Add or change the description of the macro.

Step 6: Click **OK** to save changes to the macro description or shortcut keys.

Editing Macros

Excel macros are stored in Visual Basic modules and edited in the Visual Basic Editor.

To edit a macro:

Step 1: Select **Tools > Macro > Macros…**.

Step 2: The Macros dialog box will open.

Step 3: Single-click the macro to edit.

Step 4: Click **Edit**.

Step 5: Microsoft Visual Basic opens in a new window.

Step 6: Make changes in the Visual Basic code window.

Step 7: Click **Save**.

Step 8: Close the Visual Basic program.

To test the edit on your macro:

Step 1: Click the cell in which to run the macro.

Step 2: Select **Tools > Macro > Macros…**.

Step 3: The Macros dialog box will open.

Step 4: Single-click the updated macro.

Step 5: Click **Run**.

Assigning a Macro to a Command Button

An easy way to access a macro is to place a command button on a toolbar. Instead of having to select **Tools > Macro > Macros**, selecting the macro to use, and then clicking **Run**, all you have to do is click a button on a toolbar.

To assign a macro to a command button:

Step 1: Select **View > Toolbars > Customise…**.

Step 2: The Customise dialog box opens.

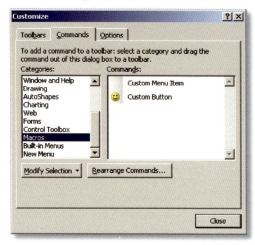

Step 3: Click the **Commands** tab.

Step 4: From the **Categories:** field, select **Macros**.

Step 5: In the **Commands:** field, select **Custom Button**.

Step 6: Click and hold the **Custom Button** icon and drag it to the **Formatting** toolbar. A thick, black line will appear on the toolbar as you move the mouse over it. The black line indicates the insertion point of the new macro button.

Step 7: Release the mouse where the macro button is to be added.

Step 8: The macro button will appear on the toolbar.

Step 9: Do not close the Customise dialog box. Right-click the new button.

Step 10: From the **Shortcut** menu, select **Assign Macro…**.

Step 11: Click the macro and click **OK**.

To change the button icon:

Step 1: Right-click the new button.

Step 2: From the **Shortcut** menu, select **Change Button Image**.

Step 3: A menu of icons will appear. Click the icon you want to use.

To edit the button icon:

Step 1: Right-click the new button.

Step 2: From the Shortcut menu, select **Edit Button Image…**.

Step 3: The Button Editor dialog box will open.

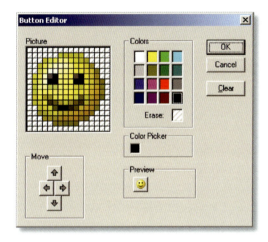

Step 4: Click any colour, and then click the image. The image changes each time you click the mouse.

Step 5: Click **OK**.

Step 6: Close the Customise dialog box.

Step 7: Test your macro by clicking the new button.

Summary

The key points discussed in this lesson are:

◆ Excel allows you to record macros to automate commonly used functions.

◆ You can quickly and easily run and edit macros.

◆ Excel also allows you to assign a macro to a command button.

Using Multiple Workbooks

Excel 2003 provides many timesaving features, such as creating and using a workspace. In addition, Excel provides tools to create workbooks that can be used simultaneously by a variety of users and automatically updated with the latest information.

Objectives

Upon completing this lesson, you will be able to:

- ✔ Use a workspace
- ✔ Link workbooks
- ✔ Preview and print multiple worksheets

Using a Workspace

Creating a workspace file is a timesaving way of working with a specific group of workbooks that you use frequently. A workspace file saves information regarding all open workbooks' locations on the screen, the size of the application window, and drive and folder locations. Opening a saved workspace file opens all workbooks in the workspace.

To create a workspace:

Step 1: Open all Excel workbooks to be included in the workspace.

Step 2: Make sure the workbook windows are arranged and sized in the exact position you want them when you open the workspace later.

Step 3: Select **File > Save Workspace…**.

Step 4: Select the location to save the workspace.

Step 5: Name the workspace file, and then click **Save**.

Linking Workbooks

Linking workbooks can be useful when working multi-departmentally on any given subject. By linking workbooks together, each department can independently manipulate its workbook (known as the source workbook), and the information will automatically update in the main workbook (known as the dependent workbook).

To link workbooks:

Step 1: Open both the source workbook and the dependent workbook.

Step 2: Create a formula in the dependent workbook by typing an equal sign into the cell that will become the workbook link.

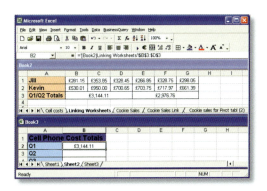

Step 3: From the source workbook, select the cell to be linked.

Step 4: Press **Enter**. You will automatically return to the dependent workbook.

Previewing and Printing Multiple Worksheets

It is easy to preview and print multiple worksheets contained within a workbook without previewing and printing the entire workbook.

To preview and print multiple worksheets:

Step 1: While holding the **Ctrl** key, click the sheet tabs of the workbooks to print. The sheet tabs will turn white, indicating that multiple sheets are grouped.

Step 2: Select **File > Print Preview**.

Step 3: Click the **Next** and **Previous** buttons to view each worksheet selected.

Step 4: Click **Print** to print the selected worksheets.

Summary

The key points discussed in this lesson are:

◆ Excel allows you to create a workspace to save time with workbooks that you use frequently.

◆ You can link workbooks so that several departments can work on them.

◆ Excel allows you to easily preview and print multiple worksheets at once.

Troubleshooting the CD-ROM

How to Run the CD-ROM

Your CD should install automatically. If you are experiencing any problems please follow the guidelines below.

Installation on Windows XP

Ensure all programs are closed before you insert the CD.
The CD should autorun.
If not, please open **Setup.exe** on the CD.

Click on **Start Installation** (select **Create shortcut on desktop** if needed)
Click on a course title to start the course

(On first launch **Accept the Agreement** and click on the title again)

To re-start the course

Use the Course Player Icon on the desktop
Or
Go to **Start** > **Programs** > **Course Player** > **Course Player**

Or
Re-insert the CD

Installation on Windows Vista

Ensure all programs are closed before you insert the CD.
Click on **Run Setup.exe** if the CD autoruns.
Otherwise open **Setup.exe** on the CD.

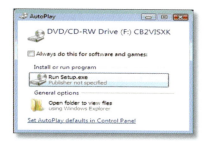

Click on **Allow** when the User Account
Control prompt comes up.

Click on **Start Installation** (select **Create
shortcut on desktop** if needed)

Click on a course title to start the course
(On first launch **Accept the Agreement** and click on the title again)

To re-start the course

Use the Course Player Icon on the desktop

Or

Go to **Start** > **All Programs** > **Course Player** > **Course Player**

Or

Re-insert the CD.

Minimum System Requirements

128 MB RAM
Windows XP or Windows Vista
Speaker and soundcard

Technical Support

If you have any problems, please e-mail us at:
techsupport@tsinteractive.com
Or
Telephone us on Freephone 00800 2667 2665 (UK & Eire).
Please ask for TS Interactive Tech Support.
For all other enquiries, visit our website: **www.tsinteractive.com**

Index